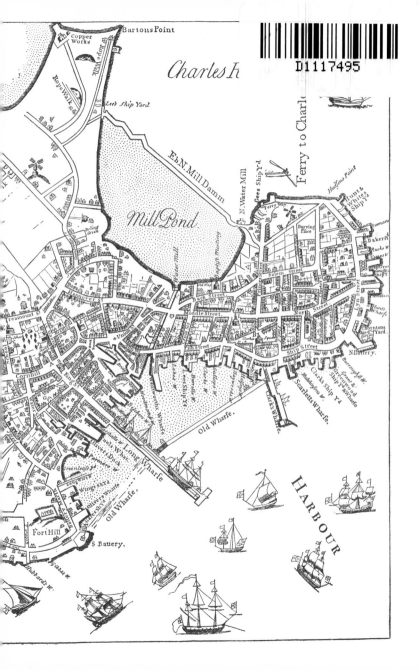

Copper Works

Bartons Point

Charles R

Leed Ship Yard

Ropewalk

E.b.N.Mill Damm

N.Water Mill

Gees Ship Yd

Ferry Way

Hudtons Point

Hunt & White's Ship Y

Ferry to Charle

Mill Pond

Bowling Green

Burying Place

German

Bakers

Rucks W

Ship Y

Hunts Wharfe

Salem Street

Hanover

North Street

Thorntons Yard

Treamount S

Cornhill

Middle Street

Fish Street

Ship Street

N.Battery

Borrough W

Gray & Co. Ship Yd & Wharfe

Charles Ship Yd

King S

Unity

Hutchinson W

Greene's Ship Y

Scarletts Wharfe.

Charles Wharfe.

Old Wharfe.

Long Wharfe

Little W

Mefis Wharfe

Roebuck Wharf

Minot's Dock

Greenlefs W

Wing's S.Yd

Old Wharfe.

HARBOUR

Fort Hill

S Battery.

Hubbard's W.

Boston

Boston

HENRY CABOT LODGE

Abridged and Illustrated

LEVENGER
PRESS

Delray Beach, Florida

Published by Levenger Press
420 South Congress Avenue
Delray Beach, Florida 33445 USA
800.544.0880
www.Levengerpress.com

Preface © 2004 the Levenger Company

This edition is an abridgment of the 1891 edition published by
Longmans, Green, and Co.
The endpaper map is from this earlier edition.

Library of Congress Cataloging-in-Publication Data

Lodge, Henry Cabot, 1850-1924.
  Boston / Henry Cabot Lodge.– Abridged ed.
      p. cm.
  "This edition is an abridgment of the 1891 edition published by
Longmans, Green, and Co."–T.p. verso.
  ISBN 1-929154-16-X
  1. Boston (Mass.)–History. I. Title.
F73.3.L63 2004
974.4'61–dc22

                                        2004001331

Cover and book design by Levenger Studios
Mim Harrison, Editor

Contents

Publisher's Preface

And this is good old Boston
The home of the bean and the cod,
Where the Lowells talk to the Cabots,
And the Cabots talk only to God.

And so the famous send-up of the Boston Brahmin lives on. But surely the Cabot of this book speaks to all of us who have ever wondered just what was meant by America's Puritan ethic and why, in today's indulgent society, we still feel its restraints.

Come tour Henry Cabot Lodge's *Boston*, and you'll soon know why.

Lodge's family, on the Cabot side, was one of the first to come to New England's shores, seafarers and merchants who settled in Salem in 1700 and later found their way to Boston. Most of the history he writes about here are events his family bore witness to. His great-grandfather, George Cabot, was a friend of George Washington's and became a U. S. senator from Massachusetts in 1791. Two years and a century later, Henry Cabot Lodge followed in his footsteps, serving in the Senate until his death in 1924.

Publisher's Preface

Born in Boston in 1850, Henry Cabot Lodge studied and later taught at Harvard. A highly regarded historian, he was a biographer of Daniel Webster, Alexander Hamilton and his great-grandfather's old friend Washington.

In *Boston*, he gives us more than the events that shaped the city's growth. He explains, as perhaps only one of its first families could, why those unyielding Puritans could create a city where independent thinking would thrive.

Boston's love for learning had a seismic effect on America, reaching all the way to California, where I was raised. Years later, it would be in Belmont, a suburb of Boston, that my wife, Lori, and I would found our company of "tools for serious readers."

So come learn more about good old Boston. Maybe you were born there, maybe not. Regardless—you may find that where there is a love of learning and of reading, there is a bit of the bean and the cod in us all.

– Steve Leveen

First Settlement of Boston

1. Founding the Town.

AMONG THE towns of which the history is told in this series, Boston in Massachusetts seems very modern. Yet these ancient towns of England are but of yesterday, when we place them beside the cities of Greece and Italy; and even the story of London itself, reaching, in tradition at least, from the days of Caesar to those of Victoria, would cover but a modest period in the long roll of the centuries witnessed by the Temple of Bubastis. The fact is that this is a comparative world, and the antiquity of races of men, or of their dwelling-places, depends altogether on the standard by which we determine age. In the United States, if we except New York, Boston is the oldest of the European settlements on the North American continent which has neither been abandoned nor remained, as at the beginning, a small town, but which has grown steadily with the growth of the country. To travellers from England, although Boston in its older part looks like many towns in their native land which have risen into importance in the last two hundred and fifty years, it seems nevertheless essentially modern. To inhabitants of the Western States, on the other hand, who have never been out of their own country, Boston seems a very ancient place indeed; and its crooked streets, where men have walked for more than two centuries, fill them with a curious interest, in which the respect that antiquity inspires is not unmingled with pity for a population which is not convulsed by a census, and for a city which is not laid out exclusively on right angles. Age, moreover, may be reckoned in another way than by years. On the sound principle laid down in Lord Tennyson's familiar line, that fifty years of Europe are better than a cycle of Cathay, the age and historic interest of a town may be judged best by events, and by the part it has played on the wider field of national life, and in the advance of what is called civilization. In this view Boston, again with the exception of New York, is the ripest in age of any of the towns or cities in the United States. In the political events which have affected the history of the entire country, and in shaping the thought of a people who have come to be a great nation, Boston has played a leading part. Much has been crowded into her two hundred and fifty years, and

> *The respect that antiquity inspires is not unmingled with pity for a city which is not laid out exclusively on right angles.*

in that time the town has lived a long life. In years alone, therefore, does Boston differ essentially from the other towns chronicled in this series. Yet this shortcoming, if it be one, is not without its advantages, for it enables us to go back to the beginning of things; to observe the origin of the community thus gathered together, and to understand the sources of its strength and of such influence as it may have had in the world.

It is to-day but little more than two hundred and fifty years since the spot where Boston now stands was an unbroken wilderness. It is not possible, nor would it probably be very profitable, to know who the first Europeans actually were who gazed upon the fair harbour, with its wooded islands, its winding river, and its background of blue hills hemming in the little peninsula where a dense and busy population is now gathered. The Norsemen, pushing southward from Iceland, probably visited that region, and some persons think that they can even identify the spots in the neighbourhood of Boston where the old sea-kings landed and lived. But if they came at all, they passed away and, so far as we know, left no trace, so that they have neither value nor interest except as agreeable subjects of antiquarian discussion. Centuries elapsed after the period of the Norse adventurers, and then the Cabots ran down the coast, glancing perhaps into the harbour, and laying the foundation of the title to the largest territory ever conquered and held by the English-speaking race. Other navigators followed in their wake at various times; but it was not until the seventeenth century had begun that the impending wave of European settlement and conquest really drew near. Then it was that the hardy Dutch skippers rounded Cape Cod— reaching out like a bended arm into the sea—and explored the coast; making rude maps, and laying the groundwork for claims of ownership on their own part which proved less perfect than those of the Cabots, for more reasons than one. Then, too, came Captain John Smith, hero of many adventures, and of many books of his own writing. He also skirted the coast of New England, looked with some care into Boston Harbour, made a map,—very creditably indeed considering his opportunities,—and then sailed away again, after christening the headlands and rivers, and laying, by his voyage, a much better foundation for permanent occupation than either his Dutch cousins or the earlier navigators.

The van of those who were actually to enter in and take possession of the land was indeed not far behind him. Five years after his voyage, the little band of men and women famous in history as the "Pilgrims" reached Cape Cod, made their compact in the cabin of the "Mayflower," and then crossing the bay founded their settlement at Plymouth. The following year in the lovely weather of early autumn, a party of them under Miles Standish made the first real exploration of Boston Harbour. They touched at some of the islands and headlands, pushed up the Mystic River, visited the deserted camps of the Indians, and traded with some of the survivors of the tribes which had been swept away by war and disease as if to leave the country open to the new comers. The Pilgrims liked the region about the harbour, but seem nevertheless to have made no serious effort to occupy it.

It was, however, too inviting a spot to remain long untouched. A little more than six months after the visit of Standish, in May, 1622, the advance-guard of a party sent out by Thomas Weston appeared, and established themselves on the southern shore of the harbour at a place called Wessagusset, now known as Weymouth. Weston was a merchant who had relations with the Plymouth people; but he was simply an adventurer and trader, and sent out his expedition solely for gain. The whole business was ill-managed, and came to a wretched end. The trading-post was abandoned, and the party dispersed.

The next effort was of a widely different character, and aimed at nothing less than the erection of a principality instead of a paltry trading-post. It was one of the numerous attempts of Sir Ferdinando Gorges, a familiar figure in the early history of New England, to carve out for himself and his children a vast domain among the unbroken forests of America. It was one of those visionary schemes—almost pathetic now, in their wild impracticability and wasted hopes—with which the new world seems to have filled the minds of adventurous men two hundred and fifty years ago. The enterprise began in all the pomp and circumstance which befitted the dreams of its projectors. The Council for New England, established under a charter granted in 1620 to the elder Gorges and thirty-nine other patentees, met at Greenwich, June 29, 1623. This charter covered the whole of the New England coast; and among the adventurers were the Dukes of Buckingham and Richmond, four earls, and many lords and gentlemen who came to Greenwich to draw lots for possessions in the new country. King James himself drew for Buckingham; and Sir Ferdinando Gorges and his son Robert were to go out at once to take possession of the new kingdom. A few weeks later in midsummer 1623 Robert Gorges sailed, commissioned as lieutenant of the Council, with full powers, civil, military, and ecclesiastical. He was to settle in the neighbourhood of Plymouth, absorb those unconsidered sectaries who were really laying the foundations of a nation, and begin the administration of the vast province which had been allotted to him and the rest of his associates, on paper. When he reached New England, therefore, he established himself at Wessagusset, the scene of Weston's ill-fated venture, and proceeded to look about him. The usual result followed. All the bright hopes melted rapidly away in the presence of the hard facts of the climate and the wilderness. America was not to be conquered in that way, nor by people of that sort, and Gorges seems to have done nothing positive, except to quarrel angrily with his predecessor, Thomas Weston. In the spring of 1624 he went back to England, "not having found the state of things near to answer his qualitie and condition," and shortly after died. The gorgeous array of names whose owners had gathered together before King James at Greenwich had meant nothing. Sir Ferdinando was in fact the only one really interested, and he could not carry the burden. No second party came. Some of Gorges's followers went home with him; others struggled through the winter, aided by the Plymouth people, and then returned to England; while others still remained. Few of them were of the right stuff, and the whole conception of the enterprise, indeed, was wildly wrong. There was no place for principalities nor powers in the new world, which needed hard-working men to build States, not adventurers seeking to transplant the forms and fashions of royalty and aristocracy, which withered and died as soon as they touched the rough new soil.

Royalty and aristocracy withered and died as soon as they touched the rough new soil.

Gorges's expedition, however, made the first permanent settlement on the shores of Boston harbour, for the post at Wessagusset was never wholly abandoned; and from the remnant of his people came the men who first established themselves in solitary plantations within the actual limits of what is now the city of Boston.

Two of these little settlements were made in 1625, on the shores of the bay at the head of which the future town was to stand. One was at Hull, where some men exiled from Plymouth and a few stragglers of uncertain origin gathered together. The other was formed by a trading-party under the lead of one Captain Wollaston, who settled within the limits of the present town of Quincy on a low hill near the shore, which still bears the name of the leader. Wollaston himself soon became dissatisfied and departed for Virginia, where he disposed of his indented servants and sent back for more, the trade in human beings having proved profitable. The second detachment was despatched, and then a revolt broke out among the ten men who were left, and Wollaston's representative was deposed, and driven away.

The leader of this revolution was one Thomas Morton, "of Clifford's Inn, Gent.," who perhaps had visited the country before with Weston, and who had certainly come out in Wollaston's company. He was one of the strangest of the many strange figures that flitted across the stage of early adventure and settlement in

America. With some education, and not a little literary ability, he was as clever and worthless a scamp as can well be imagined, and when he took possession of Mount Wollaston, which he named Merry Mount,—or Mare Mount,— he proceeded to enjoy himself freely after his own fashion. His followers were a drunken set, who traded spirits and ammunition with the savages, maintained apparently a harem of Indian women, and set up a May-pole, around which they celebrated the 1st of May in a wild and fantastic manner, not much resembling the English custom from which it was borrowed. It was easy to see that all the loose characters of the coast,—runaway servants, deserters from ships, and the like,— would flock eagerly to the standard thus erected, and that the motley crew collected in this way would prove a source of danger, as it already was a scandal, to their soberer neighbours in the other plantations. Accordingly, the Plymouth people proceeded from warnings to stronger measures; and in 1627 Miles Standish appeared at Mount Wollaston, captured Morton and took him to Plymouth, whence he was shipped to England. In the following year he found his way back again, only to fall immediately into stronger and less merciful hands than those of the Pilgrims. The Puritans came down upon him, dealt with him in their thorough fashion, and broke up his settlement. He had however one great advantage over both his Pilgrim and Puritan enemies, for he wrote a narrative of his adventures in a reckless and amusing fashion of which they were incapable, and thus has kept the laugh forever on his side. His worthless and picturesque career and his wild and disorderly settlement have furnished material for the imagination of Hawthorne and Motley; and while better men are forgotten, Morton and Merry Mount stand out with a glow of colour against the dark background of suffering which make up the story of the first years of New England settlement, and are still freshly remembered among the descendants of the very men who brought Morton himself to condign punishment.

The little plantations at Weymouth, Hull, and Mount Wollaston, although within the limits of Boston Bay, nevertheless do not concern us here so much as the solitary men who had made homes for themselves upon the land now actually part of the modern city. On an island in the harbour was settled David Thomson, "Gent.," an attorney for Gorges, with his family. Thomson died in 1628, leaving to his family his island and to the island his name, which it has borne ever since. On Noddle's Island, now East Boston, was established Samuel Maverick, a young gentleman of property and education, who had there laid out a farm, built him a house and fort, where four guns were mounted, and which served as a refuge and defence for all the planters of the neighbourhood. On the next peninsula, where Charlestown grew up, where the battle of Bunker Hill was fought, and which has now been absorbed by the city, was settled Thomas Walford, a blacksmith, with his family. Across the bay from Maverick and Walford, on the very spot where the future city was to rise, William Blackstone had laid out a farm and orchard, and built him a house on the western slope of one of the hills, whence he could see the sun set across the windings of the river Charles, and over the wide brown marshes through which it made its way. Blackstone was a graduate of Cambridge, a man of learning and of books, who managed apparently to bring a library with him to the wilderness, and who seems to have sought only to be silent and alone. He was another of those characters that look dimly mysterious now, and thus excite our curiosity, but which no doubt would prove commonplace enough if we could ever get them into nearer view. When new comers arrived, Puritans, for whom he had no love apparently, he withdrew to Rhode Island, and there in a solitary spot lived to be eighty years of age. His diaries were burned after his death when the Indians destroyed his house, and the mystery and story of his life, if there were any, perished.

These four early settlers of Boston were all survivors of the Gorges expedition. Of the three settled within the actual limits of the city, two were gentlemen of property and education, and all were members of the Church of England. It is a curious fact that the first settlers on the ground where that town was destined to be built which was above all others the town of the English Puritan, were all of the Church of England and of the Court party. But they were merely the driftwood of a wreck. The Court and Church had failed to conquer and possess New England, and the time was at hand when the real conquerors—men of the same race but of widely different character and creed—were to come and make the land their own.

The title under which these new comers took possession starts with the Company of Northern Virginia, which in 1620 turned over its property to the better-known Council for New England. The latter organization, heavy with much aristocracy, had a brief period of hope, and a still briefer period of prosperity due to the fisheries, and soon overclouded by French and Spanish wars. Then dividing its property in 1623, it relapsed into silence so far as records are concerned, only to emerge into a second existence, vocal but unimportant, in 1631.

In the interval of silence, however, under cover of the titles and court finery and empty parlance of the Council for New England, something real had been accomplished by people of a plainer but more effective sort. John White, clergyman of Dorchester, a man of serious mind, as men were in those days, was troubled by the godless life of those among his parishioners—and they were not a few—who were engaged in the fisheries. He conceived the scheme of forming a little settlement within the territory of the Council for New England, where fishing-crews could be better supplied with provisions, money made by trade, and religious instruction given to both the fishermen and the settlers. For this pious and frugal scheme he raised £3,000; a vessel was bought, and a fishing-station or settlement established at Cape Ann, near the present city of Gloucester. The little venture did not prosper. The money in stock melted away, no new money came in, and after three years the association dissolved their company, and sold what property they had. The causes of the failure may be learned from White himself, but they were common to new settlements, and are not now of moment.

The sinking of the little fortunes of the Dorchester Associates in the vast sea of colonial losses and mishaps would not be worth remembering were it not for the thread, slender withal, but yet distinct and strong, which connects them with successors of a very similar character. The people in England who were shortly to furnish the force to move the English world were the hard-working,

God-fearing men who took life and religion and politics very seriously, and who urged, in persistent fashion, that matters in England both in Church and State were in evil plight, and in sore need of reform. Whenever in that first half of the seventeenth century in England we come across these men, we may know that, whether wisely or unwisely, something was actually and effectually done, and that we have got clear of the court atmosphere of lies and vacillations, of halting action and unworthy ambition. In the founder of the little Dorchester company we have one of these earnest men, full of serious purpose, troubled about many things, and striving much, whom the world knows as Puritans. With such a promoter as John White there were sure to be some followers of like character; and when the little enterprise went to pieces there were four "prudent and honest men" who remained.

Earnest men, full of serious purpose, troubled about many things, and striving much, whom the world knows as Puritans.

Headed by Roger Conant, a man still clear to us as possessed of leadership and force, these four went southward and westward from Cape Ann and settled at a place called Naumkeag, to be better known in future as Salem. To these men, if they would stay, as stay they did in very manful fashion, the

Rev. John White promised aid, support, and a patent. How much he had to do with what followed is not perfectly determined, and is now of little consequence; it suffices that he kept his word.

Then during the silent period of the records of the Council for New England a patent for lands was obtained, only to be soon lost sight of and overshadowed by a royal charter. Just how this charter was secured no one has ever known; but greater forces were behind this movement than had ever been summoned as yet to any colonizing of the new world. It passed the seals March 4 1629, a date to be made widely memorable by one of its descendants; for the charter of a trading-company thus obtained was destined to become the fundamental law of a State, and the first of the written constitutions which have become the cornerstones of American systems of government. It was not by accident that the charter came to these large results. Both the charter and its purposes were part of a well-matured plan, and nearly a year before it passed the seals the promoters had fitted out an expedition under the direction of John Endicott, who established headquarters at Salem, with a commission as governor of the colony in New England. At home the company had another governor, Matthew Cradock; and he it was who in July, 1629, read certain propositions, conceived by himself, for the purpose of inducing persons of worth and quality to transfer themselves and families to the plantations. These propositions were the subject of much careful and secret consideration, and resulted, as was undoubtedly intended by the promoters, in the agreement at Cambridge, which was signed by Winthrop and Saltonstall, and other leaders, and which also resulted in the transfer of the title of the company itself to New England.

This was the last of the preliminary steps toward the establishment of an independent government in America; and the men who put their names to this agreement were persons of such standing and importance in the community as to prove beyond any doubt that no mere trading-venture or voyage of discovery was intended. The signers of the agreement were country gentlemen and merchants well born, well connected, persons of reputation and substance; while their followers whom they took with them were drawn from the hardy yeomanry of England, and from the thrifty mechanics and shopkeepers of her towns. After the arrangement had been made to transfer the charter of the company, the Court of Assistants elected a new governor in the person of John Winthrop, with Sir Richard Saltonstall, Mr. Isaac Johnson (who married the daughter of the Earl of Lincoln), and John Endicott among the assistants.

The purpose of the organization thus effected, though secret at the time, is now abundantly clear. The Puritan party were coming slowly to the conclusion that reforms in England, both in

Church and State, were impossible. With Strafford at the head of the army and Laud in control of the Church, with ship-money, forced loans, and illegal taxes, with Parliament dissolved and the king's purpose proclaimed of ruling without one, there seemed little hope in the Old World for the liberty-loving and religious men who made up the bulk of the Puritan party. For this reason they went forth to the New World to find a place of refuge for the people thus threatened and opposed. As Winthrop said, in his "Reasons to be considered for justifying the undertakers of the intended plantation in New England,"

> God hath provided this place to be a refuge for many whome he meanes to save out of the generall callamity, & seeing the church hath noe place lefte to flie into but the wildernesse, what better worke can there be, than to goe & provide tabernacles & foode for her against she comes thether.

With the charter in hand, the governor and company finally started with a small fleet of eleven or twelve ships about the 1st of April, 1630. Before going, they addressed a noble letter to those whom they left behind, in which they took leave with sorrow and affection of their country and of the Church of England, which they called their "dear mother." With this farewell they sailed; and after seventy-six days the "Arbella" and her consorts came to anchor off Salem, where Endicott received them, and turned the government over to Winthrop. There were gathered already at Salem some three hundred settlers. With Winthrop came seven or eight hundred, increased very shortly to a thousand, by some additional vessels; and this was soon after followed by a second thousand. No such attempt at settlement had been seen before on the American continent. It was not the longing for adventure, but the transfer of a people, a government, and a Church; and this it is which separates it from all other colonizing undertakings in America at their inception, and which made the Massachusetts settlement from the beginning such a moving force in American history.

The little colony at Salem had had its sufferings like its predecessor at Plymouth, and the arrival of Winthrop with his fleet was, as one may readily suppose, welcome enough; but Salem did not suit the new comers for a place of settlement and the establishment of a town. They moved farther south along the coast until they came to the spot where the village which became afterward the city of Charlestown, was planted, and which is now included in the larger city of Boston. Here they established a settlement; and on the 30th of July, Winthrop, Dudley, Johnson, and the pastor, John Wilson, adopted and signed a simple church covenant, which was the foundation of the independent churches of New England. Here too, at Charlestown, was held the first Court of Assistants; and everything seemed to point to the permanency of the town as the capital of the Puritan State. A comparatively trivial cause led to a removal. The change of climate and exposure brought its inevitable result to those unused to such trials, in the form of illness and death. Isaac Johnson died, and his wife, the Lady Arbella, as well as many others, leaders in the colony; while in addition to these sorrows, provisions grew scarce, and the springs on which they depended for water began to fail. It was this lack of water which finally drove Winthrop to leave Charlestown and establish his future city on the three-hilled peninsula across the bay.

Lack of water finally drove Winthrop to establish his future city on the three-hilled peninsula across the bay.

On the 17th of September, 1630, the removal took place, and the foundation of the new town was marked by an order of the Court of Assistants, which decreed that "Trimontaine" should be called Boston,— the good old English name of the principal town in the region whence most of the leaders and founders of the Puritan community had come.

A Prospect of the Colleges in Cambridge in New England

2. The Rise of Church and State.

THE PLACE thus finally selected for the site of the future capital of New England would have been the last chosen probably, if the settlers had been able to peer into the future, and to realize how contracted the natural limits would prove for the population destined to gather there. To their eyes, however, there must have appeared ample room and verge enough for any town they could picture to themselves, and nature had certainly made the spot fair and pleasing to all who looked upon it.

The place to which Winthrop and his followers removed, and where they built their city, was a peninsula connected on the south with the mainland by a narrow strip of ground which just prevented it from being an island. This strip was known as the "Neck" and continues to bear that title, although the process of filling up on each side has taken all meaning from the name. On the west of the "Neck" were long reaches of flats and marshes covered by the tides at high water, and known to the inhabitants of Boston for more than two hundred years as the Back Bay.

Beyond the flats was the Charles River, sweeping down to the peninsula, and dividing it from the mainland on the north and

On the west of the "Neck" were long reaches of flats and marshes known as the Back Bay.

east as the stream broadened first into a great inlet and then at last united with the sea. On the east the peninsula came boldly down into the harbour, and as one followed its line to the south, the "Neck" was reached once more, with marshes again between it and deep water. Modern energy and the demands of a growing population have dyked and filled all these flats and marshes, and covered them with houses, the Back Bay becoming the west end of the city, where wealth and fashion have gone to dwell on gravel spread over the space once claimed by the tides and inhabited only by sea-birds. On the main part of the peninsula the land rose abruptly into three small hills, which fell away toward the harbour in gentle slopes. Here the settlers built their houses, sheltered by the hills from the cold winds of the north and west, and looking out upon the ocean to the southeast. Wharves were soon run out into the deep harbour, which afforded an excellent and safe anchorage, and thence from the water's edge the town began to grow, moving westward over the hills behind.

Boston

The Puritans of Massachusetts, after the usual fashion of their race, were at bottom intensely conservative, lovers of law and order, and believers in authority. At the same time they had very well-defined views of their own as to what ought to be done in Church and State in England, and now they suddenly found themselves with nothing to reform, and able to set up unhampered by any restrictions just such a government and just such churches as they believed England ought to have. This vast liberty did not lead them into license or into fanciful experiments, but none the less it had, as was inevitable, an immediate and powerful influence upon them. They were driven forward upon the road marked out for them by their own beliefs with the irresistible force of circumstances. To the Puritans of that day, religion and a belief in God were living realities so vivid and forceful that they overrode and made trivial every other thought.

Only religious men and good men were to be freemen and voters in the new commonwealth, and religion and goodness were determined by membership in the church. Within the pale of the church it was a plain democratic government, both in things spiritual and things temporal, where all were equal in the sight of God and the law. But to the outsiders dwelling under the government of the Massachusetts Bay Company the rule was that of a religious oligarchy, where the clergy determined a man's fitness both in religion and in politics, an enormous power, which, even after its reality had gone, continued for more than a century to exercise a dominating influence in New England. So long as the great body of citizens were members of the church, and therefore freemen of the State, no very serious difficulty was likely to arise; but the moment of trial was sure to come when a large minority existed who were deprived of political power because they did not stand inside the pale of the church.

Within the single limitation thus imposed, the development in political institutions went forward with great rapidity. At the third General Court, held in Boston in 1632, it was agreed that the governor, deputy-governor, and assistants should be chosen by the whole court including both assistants and freemen, thus recognizing always within the bounds of the church, the democratic principle, another vast stride from the political system they had left behind, and yet again a step which seemed perfectly natural and, in the new conditions, unavoidable. At the same session of the court it was ordered that two of every plantation should be appointed to confer with the court about the raising of a public stock; and accordingly two persons were appointed from each of the eight little settlements which had sprung up in the neighbourhood of Boston. Here again was the planting of a principle quite as memorable as that which united Church and

State in one, and gave a vote to all the freemen; for this provision established once and for all in New England the doctrine that no one should be taxed without direct representation in the body imposing the taxes. In the following year the idea thus planted was expanded into a more definite form of regular representation by an order that there should be four General Courts every year, but that the whole body of freemen should be present only at the court for the election of magistrates, while to the other three each town should send deputies, who should assist in making laws and in governing the Commonwealth. This not only established representative government, as will be seen, but it also recognized the existence of the unit of the political structure of New England in the shape of the township.

The New England township was the corner-stone of the fabric of New England government. It was formed by a group of persons settling together in a given spot, and taking up a certain amount of land for farming and other purposes. By a curious process of reversion the Englishmen thus settled in the new world revived in a marked degree the ancient principles of communal property in land which their earliest progenitors had practised in the forests of Germany before they set out on their career of conquest. In many of these New England towns, pasture and woodland were owned in common; and each citizen of the town had certain rights of pasture for sheep or cattle, and certain rights of cutting wood, which descended like other property from father to son. These communal holdings have gradually disappeared, but a few have survived even to the present day, a curious monument of the fixity of habits of thought, and of the survival of the most ancient institutions in the midst of the rushing life of modern democracy. The other lands of the town, house-lots and farming lands, were held in severalty. The houses of the farmers were clustered together, for the most part, near the village meeting-house, while the lands which they farmed stretched about them in all directions to the limits of the township.

More important, however, than communal rights or methods of farming was the system of town government. All the citizens of the town assembled in general meeting once a year or oftener, levied taxes, decided on improvements, and appointed the necessary executive officers to carry out their behests during the ensuing twelve months. In the town meeting all men met on an equality; every citizen was entitled to free speech and a free vote, and no purer democracy, no more absolute example of a people governing themselves, has ever been devised. So long as the towns remained small, property equally distributed, and moderate in amount, and the interests of the people few and simple, this method of government was as practical as it was admirable. When however the communities thus gathered together reached too great a population for the single assembly, they were obliged to pass out of the stage of the town meeting into a representative municipal government, although this change did not begin until the first quarter of the present century was well-nigh spent.

It was in the town meeting that every New Englander became accustomed to deal with public affairs. It was there that he learned to be a politician and a debater; and it was there also that the principle of union and of federation was taught, because the union of the towns

In the town meeting all men met on an equality; no purer democracy has ever been devised.

made the State, and from that it was but a step to understand that the union of States would make a nation. The town organization was also one of great political force. The difficulty of combining a sparse population in any political movement was never felt in New England, as in many others of the American colonies. Her people were from the outset banded together in compact groups, and these groups were in turn welded together into a commonwealth. The power of political action in the New England townships was one of the great factors which separated the colonies from England; and even as late as 1809 it was the action of the New

England towns which shook the country, forced the repeal of the embargo, and sent Jefferson, who had always feared and admired them, into a retirement which was clouded by defeat and disappointment after all his years of triumph.

While with one hand the Puritans set up the most rigid religious tests, with the other they planted the purest democracy ever seen.

The system of town government was the same in Boston as in the smallest and remotest village; and what was true of one was true of all. Thus it came to pass that while with one hand the Puritans set up a political system which rested on the most rigid religious tests, with the other they planted in the government of town and State, the purest democracy which has ever been seen.

At this very time also the records of Boston disclose the planting of another principle quite as important as that adopted either in religion or politics; for it was then generally agreed that "Brother Philemon Pormont shalbe entreated to become schollmaster for the teaching and nourtering of children with us." Three years later all the principal inhabitants subscribed for the maintenance of a free school, and at the same time the General Court laid the foundation of Harvard College.

In this way was founded a system of free public-schools which spread to every town in the Commonwealth, and with them a college was established for the purposes of a higher education. Thus the Puritans arranged that a narrow creed should be the only test of citizenship, and on one side of it they placed a democratic government and on the other free schools. They fettered the human mind with their religious doctrines, while by their system of education and politics they struck off every shackle which could impede the march of thought. That they were aware of the profound contradiction which underlay this system cannot be supposed. But whether they realized it or not, they had yoked together three principles which sooner or later must come into conflict. The history of Massachusetts is the history of the development of these principles, and of the final triumph of the two which made for freedom over the one which repressed all liberty except within its own narrow bounds.

From the beginning it seems to have been assumed by the Puritans that they should exercise an absolute power in determining who should dwell within their boundaries, with the right to expel any person whose presence they deemed prejudicial to the welfare of Church or State. They had used this authority in the case of Morton and other obscure but disorderly persons whom they deemed harmful from a secular point of view, and also in the case of the Browns, who seemed to be hostile to the religious establishment projected by the Puritans. Their theory, however, was soon to be put to a much severer test. Among those who came to Boston in 1631 was Roger Williams, a clergyman, and even then a man of some repute. He was asked to act as teacher at the First Church in the absence of Wilson, but declined because the members would not make humble confession of sin for having communed with the Church of England. From Boston he went to Salem, where he met with some success, then to Plymouth, where he was not equally fortunate, and thence he returned to Salem in 1634, the Plymouth people fearing that if he remained "he would run a course of rigid Separation and Anabaptistry." By this time his views had become more pronounced, and he undertook to deny the right of the magistrate to act outside of civil matters, and to question the rights of the colonists to their lands under the charter as against the savages. This states the cause of his offending in the language of his champions; but no statement can disguise the fact that these declarations whether right or wrong, whether the utterances of a seditious agitator or the pleadings of a noble spirit in favour of soul-liberty, struck at the very foundations of the State which had been established. He was therefore sentenced by the General Court to depart out of their jurisdiction within six weeks; but being allowed to stay till spring he continued to propagate his doctrines, and seven days after the "more firm and friendly uniting of minds" among the magistrates and ministers, Captain Underhill was despatched to seize him and ship him to England. Williams however escaped, and made his way to the Narragansett country, where he founded what afterward became the colony of Rhode Island, and thus passed out of the history of Boston.

It is as easy as it is familiar, in this connection, to denounce the Puritans of Massachusetts as harsh and unfeeling bigots, who persecuted and banished the liberal and open-minded spirits who came among them. But it is too often forgotten that at that period the world, according to our conceptions, was a narrow and bigoted world, in which differences in religious opinion were supposed to go to the very roots of everything. It is not remembered, moreover, that the Puritans did not come to Massachusetts to obtain for everybody "freedom to worship God," but to get freedom to worship God in their own particular way. They were reformers at home, not Separatists; and when they landed in Massachusetts, although they did not attempt to copy the Church which they had left, it never occurred to their minds that any Christian State worth having could exist without an established Church of some kind, because that was a condition of affairs quite outside the range of their experience.

They accordingly established a Church of their own, and made it one with their State, while hand in hand with the establishment of this religious State went the building up of the body politic. Whoever touched the one touched the other, and according to the Puritan theory was to be dealt with unhesitatingly by the strong arm of the civil power.

In 1641 the "Body of Liberties," or code of laws, was adopted by the people of Massachusetts. A very memorable code it was, in which may be found the germ of many of the great principles of legislation upon which American government rests today. During this time, too, another political question was settled which also had an important bearing upon American methods of transacting public business. Boston by that time had grown sufficiently to have streets; and wandering through those streets and pastures, in 1636, there was discovered a stray sow, which was taken and held by the finder, Captain Keayne. Then, after many months, the owner appeared; and thence grew a mighty dispute which was carried into the General Court, and which resulted in the division of the General Court into two houses, one of magistrates and the other of deputies.

In 1643, however, the year before this legislative division took place, a much greater event occurred, and one fruitful of interest to the student of American history; for in that year was formed the New England Confederation or Union, consisting of the four colonies of Massachusetts, Plymouth, New Haven, and Connecticut. It would be inappropriate to enter here into any discussion of this far-reaching subject, or to trace the history of the New England Confederation which made these four colonies a great power at the time, and which served as an example for a similar union upon a much larger scale. But no history of Boston would be complete without noting that the little Congress composed of the representatives of the four colonies met at Boston on Sept. 17, 1643, and there planted the federal principle of government which on Sept. 17, 1787, was again given to the world in the Constitution of the United States.

During these years, too, relations were opened with the other colonies on the Atlantic seaboard, and the trade of Boston stretched out in every direction north and south.

During all this political and material progress the work of education went on. In 1642, the first Commencement was held at Harvard College, where "nine young men of good hope performed their acts so as to give good proof of their proficiency in the tongues and arts." In 1645, we find in Winthrop's Journal that "divers free schools were erected," and that Boston made an order to allow forever fifty pounds and a house to the master, and thirty pounds and a house to an usher,—an example rapidly followed by the other towns. Two years later the free school was made the subject of a general law of the Commonwealth. It was then ordered that as it was "one chief project of that old deluder Satan to keep men from the knowledge of the Scriptures…every township in this jurisdiction after the Lord hath increased them to the number of fifty householders shall then forthwith appoint one within their town to teach all such children as shall resort to him to write and read;" and it was further ordered that when "any town shall increase to the number of one hundred families they shall set up a grammar school the master thereof being able to instruct youth so far as they may be fitted for the university." No nobler legislation than this is to be found in the laws of any infant State; but the men who framed it were blind to the fact that such legislation made impossible the religious system which they had also set up.

Two years later John Winthrop died. He had prevailed over every attack made upon him, and he died in the fulness of his fame and popularity, mourned and beloved by the entire Commonwealth. Winthrop had shown himself to be a really great man,—one who took high rank in that small class of the founders of States, whose achievements have been most difficult and at the same time of most value to their fellowmen. He was buried with "great solemnity and honor" in what is now known as the King's Chapel burying ground. Under his leadership and influence the lines on which the Puritan State was to move had been all marked out. The next stage in the history of Boston shows the passage of the Puritan town and colony through the period of Puritan ascendency and decline in the English-speaking world until after much suffering and tribulation the quiet of the provincial time was reached.

A Prospective View of part of the Commons
(as it would be in 1768)

3. The Defence of the Charter.

THE FOUNDATIONS of the future city had been well laid, and so had those of the Church and State, during the period when Winthrop had guided and formulated the policy of Massachusetts. The work which was then begun under his wise leadership moved forward in things spiritual and political as well as in material affairs without break or change. That which most concerns us during the ten years after Winthrop's death, when John Endicott held the reins of government, is the culmination of the struggle between the stern theocracy which had been established with so much care and the spirit of toleration and liberal thought which was rising up from the free schools and the democratic commonwealth. The persecution of the Baptists, which was carried on for some years after Winthrop's death, resulted in failure. These Baptists, however, were much less difficult to deal with and much better able to win toleration than the people called Quakers, who succeeded them, and before whom the Puritan system of repression in reality broke down, although the fact of its defeat was not realized until the appearance of outside political forces made it painfully evident to all men.

This is not the place to enter into a detailed history of the Quaker persecution. It has been the fashion in these days to represent the case as if all the wrong were on one side, and all human sympathy should be with the Quakers. It seldom happens in any quarrel that all the wrong is on one side. Life would be much simpler if such were the case. In this instance wrong was largely on one side, but not entirely so. The Quakers, whom the world has known for the past two centuries as quiet, law-abiding, and benevolent citizens, were very different from those who came and set themselves up against the authorities of Massachusetts. These early agitators, apart from their religious doctrines, and considered solely from the secular standpoint, were offensive and disorderly persons, as unlike the seraphic beings of modern poetry and history as can well be imagined. Their cause was righteous, no doubt, but they were not by any means. Men and women who raised disturbances in the streets, went about without clothes, smearing their bodies with black, who denounced the civil magistrates and the law, who broke into the midst of peaceful congregations, and indulged in every sort of indecent performance, would in these days of enlightened liberality be placed in jail for disorderly and indecent conduct; and the present generation would feel that they had been treated with absolute justice as law-breakers and disturbers of the peace.

If the Puritans had treated the Quakers solely from the secular standpoint, made them keep order, and inflicted upon them nothing more than the usual punishments for infraction of the law, it would be very difficult to say that they had acted otherwise than as sensible men. Unfortunately, they could never keep matters of conscience and opinion separate from overt acts; and that which offended the Puritan most was the fact that the "Ranters," as they called them, were not only disorderly persons but people who held religious views at variance with those of the State. Feeling in this way, the Puritan authorities undertook to suppress the Quakers as religious fanatics instead of simply punishing them as disturbers of the peace. Even Roger Williams, the conventional champion of soul-liberty and of freedom of conscience, declared himself in favour of due and moderate restraint and punishment of the Quakers; and if the Puritans had kept themselves to this, all would have been well. Unluckily they went much further. They undertook to extirpate them; and they adopted in so doing the repression to which they were accustomed, and used methods which were neither better nor worse in Massachusetts than the methods of punishment then in vogue everywhere. They imprisoned the Quakers, whipped them at the cart-tail from town to town, and banished them from the jurisdiction of the Commonwealth under pain of death, a system which on the whole had thus far proved fairly effective. This,

Between 1659 and 1661 three men and one woman were executed on Boston Common, where they still lie buried.

time, however, they were dealing with men and women so crazed by religious feeling that they were ready to meet even the last penalty in order to establish their faith. The Quakers came back from exile to find that the Puritans, whatever their faults, were men of their word. Between 1659 and 1661 three men and one woman were executed on Boston Common, where it is believed they still lie buried. It was with great difficulty that a majority of the magistrates could be obtained to carry out the threat that had been made; and it may be doubted whether the policy would have prevailed if it had not been for the unbending will of stern old Governor Endicott, who in his earlier days had cut the cross from the English flag as a symbol of idolatry. The victory in appearance rested with the magistrates, but in reality the Puritan system of a single church had broken down. Public opinion was so strongly excited by the execution of the Quakers that the policy it embodied could never again have been carried out thoroughly. It was the last victory of the theocratic system of the founders, and is of profound interest because it shows that system carried out to its logical conclusion, and failing in the end in the presence of the modern forces which were being generated by free schools and a free government.

In 1660, Charles II. came back to his father's throne; and the ship that brought the news of the Restoration to Boston brought also the two regicides, Goffe and Whalley, fleeing from the wrath to come. Within a year the "Colonels," as they were called, who had been on their arrival the honoured guests of the State, were hiding in remote places with a price upon their heads, and Massachusetts heard that her former governor, Sir Henry Vane, and her great preacher, Hugh Peter, had died upon the scaffold. It was evident that this was a government which, unlike that of Richard Cromwell, could not be passed over without some acknowledgment; and they therefore sent what they called a "congratulatory and lowly script," acknowledging Charles, and asking for his protection.

Charles returned a gracious although vague reply to the address of the colony; but despite the fair words, signs were not wanting to anxious observers in Massachusetts that the home Government was planning to take a much more effective control of their affairs than they either liked or expected. The Navigation Act of Cromwell, which had never been enforced against them under the Protectorate, was recommended by the Convention Parliament to be made more stringent and was put into active operation. Twelve privy councilors were also appointed to be a commission touching the settlement of New England. This was in May, 1661; and while the Government in England was thus gradually turning its attention to the Puritan colonies, the General Court of Massachusetts at the same time was appointing a committee of twelve to take into consideration the present condition of affairs. This committee made a report in June, which set forth the rights of the colony under the charter, and secondly the duties of allegiance which the colonists owed the

The Massachusetts Government proclaimed the king in Boston, fifteen months after his accession, — a delay which certainly did not indicate an over-hasty loyalty.

king. The clauses in this report "concerning our liberties" were very definite and very broad, while those concerning allegiance were vague, and did not extend very far, a distinction not likely to escape observant and hostile eyes. Having thus set forth their own ideas of their rights and duties much as if they were entering a *caveat*, the Massachusetts Government, in August, 1661, proclaimed the king in Boston, fifteen months after his accession,—a delay which certainly did not indicate an over-hasty loyalty. The news which came to them, however, convinced them that more active steps should be taken to defend their rights in England than the reports of committees or tardy proclamations of the existence of the reigning king; and after much deliberation Mr. Bradstreet and Mr. Norton left the colony in February, 1662, as agents of the colony, to represent its interests in London. Yet at this very time, when agents were being sent with no little anxiety, the colony continued to exercise one of the highest attributes of independent sovereignty, by continuing the coinage of money. Their deeds were by no means so submissive as their words. Nevertheless, the agents were well received in England, and returned with a letter from the king dated June 28, 1662. This letter was more gracious and liberal than the colonists ought to have expected; for Charles told the Massachusetts Government that their address had been very acceptable; that he received the colony into his gracious protection, confirmed their charter, and was ready to renew it; and that he pardoned all subjects for offences against him, except persons attainted for high treason,— the exception referring to fugitive regicides.

After such concessions and such apparent liberality, the king on his side demanded certain things which seemed very grievous to the Puritans of Massachusetts, who had been carrying on for so long an independent government. Charles directed that the oath of allegiance should be observed, and that the administration of justice should be in his name; and as a feature of the charter was freedom of conscience, he charged that they should extend that freedom to all members of the Episcopal Church. He also directed that all freeholders of good character and orthodox in religion, though of different persuasions concerning church and government, should be allowed to vote. This last command struck of course at the very root of the Puritan system; and when the General Court met in October, 1662, the only thing they did was to direct that all writs should run in the king's name, while at the next session, in May, 1663, they appointed a committee to consider the rest of the letter. The colonists were quite ready to go through all the forms of obedience; but when it came to substantial concessions they grew straightway stubborn, and began to play the waiting game, which had always served them so well.

Meanwhile the Committee of the Privy Council had begun to move; and in April, 1663, it was declared that his Majesty had determined to send new commissioners to the colonies to preserve the charter of the Plantation, and to remove existing differences. The news that these men were coming as passengers on men-of-war, and accompanied by troops, reached Massachusetts in the spring of 1664. When the General Court met in May, it appointed Captains Oliver and Davis to go on board these ships as soon as they appeared, and to acquaint the commissioners that the officers and soldiers should be permitted to land only in small numbers, and unarmed. The Court also appointed a day of humiliation and prayer, gave the patent and its duplicate to certain persons to be hidden in a safe and secret place, ordered the trainbands to be put in readiness, and placed Captain Davenport in command of the castle in the harbour. Thus prepared, both spiritually and temporally, they awaited the coming of the ships. Two of the men-of-war reached Boston on the 23d of July, 1664, and the others followed. The fleet

When it came to substantial concessions they grew straightway stubborn, and began to play the waiting game, which had always served them so well.

brought some four hundred troops for the reduction of the Dutch settlements and four commissioners—Colonel Nichols, Sir Robert Carr, Colonel Cartwright, and Mr. Maverick. These gentlemen bore the royal commission, which ordered them to reduce the Dutch of New York, to hear all trials of complaint against existing governments, and to settle the peace and security of the country. They also brought a letter from the king which gave a more detailed expression of the powers set out in the commission.

The commissioners laid before the governor's council their commission and the king's letter, and asked for men to assist them in the reduction of New York, whither they went at once, after stating in broad terms that they would return later and hoped for a more satisfactory answer than the king's missives had yet received. When the General Court assembled in August they resolved that they would keep true faith and allegiance to his Majesty, and also would adhere to the patent. They gave two hundred men for service against the Dutch and then proceeded to consider the king's letter of 1662, which they had had before them for two years. By way of compliance with its requests they repealed the law which confined the franchise to church membership and replaced it by another, which gave a vote to those who, with certain other unimportant qualifications, could present a certificate from the minister of the place where they lived that they were orthodox in religion. This was a change without a difference; and the practical effect of this new law was the same as the old, for it left the control of the franchise in the hands of the ministers.

The commissioners came back to Massachusetts in February, and proceeded thence to Plymouth, Rhode Island, and Connecticut, where they met with a reception or a submission which was satisfactory to them and to the king. By the following May they were once more in Boston, prepared for the last contest. John Endicott, sternest and most unyielding of all the Puritan magistrates, had died, and had been succeeded by Richard Bellingham; but the policy of the colony was unchanged. When the opponents were at last fairly face to face there ensued a plentiful exchange of letters and much discussion, none of which tended to any results. After a good deal of irritation on both sides the commissioners decided to bring the conflict to a direct issue. They accordingly announced that they would hold a court, at which the colony was cited to appear as defendant, at the house of Captain Bridger, on Hanover Street, in Boston, at nine o'clock in the morning of May 24, 1665. The General Court of the colony was prepared for this move. At eight o'clock in the morning on the appointed day a messenger of the Court appeared in front of Captain Bridger's house, blew an alarm on his trumpet, and proclaimed in his Majesty's name and by authority of the royal charter that it regarded this action of the commissioners as a gross usurpation, which could not be countenanced or allowed. Then the messenger and trumpeter went to other parts of the little town and with similar ceremony made the same proclamation. Thus it befell that when the commissioners assembled at nine o'clock on the same morning they found nobody either to hear them or to confer with, except Colonel Cartwright, who was ill with the gout in Captain Bridger's house, and who had had the pleasure of listening at an early hour to the trumpeter and the proclamation. So far as the commissioners were concerned the matter was at an end, for they had no force sufficient to cope with that of the colony. Accordingly they stated that they would not lose more of their labours in so unpromising a field, and thereupon departed.

In this first struggle with the Crown, Massachusetts triumphed; and having triumphed, the colonists proceeded to show their loyalty in their own way, by sending provisions to the royal fleet in the West Indies and masts for the navy to England. Meantime chance favoured them. Other matters intervened, and another decisive struggle was not destined to come for some years. In the following year a letter came from the king through Maverick, directing the Government to send four or five persons to attend upon his Majesty, which the General Court, with great humility, declined to do, and then proceeded to send out the gifts of provisions and masts, which were much needed and well received. The first attempt of the government of the Restoration to take control of Massachusetts had been scattered by the blast of the trumpeter of the General Court.

Seat of King Philip

4. King Philip's War, and the Loss of the Charter.

THUS THE contest ended for the time, but it was only for the time, and owing to particular conditions. England just then had other matters to think of than the New England colonies, and so for ten years the political relations between Massachusetts and the mother country were almost nothing. Still the contumacious colonies were never wholly forgotten, for complaints were continually made against them in regard to the violation of the Navigation Act, and Gorges and Mason continued to press their claims to the territory of Maine and New Hampshire, thus keeping alive the memory of the stubborn disobedience of the distant American Puritans. Finally the Privy Council came to a decision in regard to the various complaints and suggestions, and once more entered upon an active policy in regard to New England. One Edward Randolph, who was destined to play an important part in Boston during the next few years, a tool of the Court, and possessed of much talent for spying and intrigue, was sent out as an agent to Massachusetts in March, 1673, with copies of the petitions and complaints of Mason and Gorges.

He landed in Boston in June, 1676, to begin his work; but the full meaning of his mission was hardly appreciated at the moment, for evil as his coming was, a worse, and a far more ferocious enemy than he could be was already upon the colony.

Just a year before Randolph's arrival, on the 21st of June, 1675, a messenger from Marshfield—a little town to the southward—had galloped into Boston bearing a letter from Governor Winslow of Plymouth to Governor Leverett. Since the thorough slaughter of the early days at the Pequot fort, in the language of the old chronicler, "the land had rested forty years;" but this messenger riding through Boston streets in hot haste brought tidings that the long quiet was at last broken, and that the most desolating Indian war which the colony would ever know, had begun. Winslow had not asked for troops, but none the less the town was astir at once over the news, and knew well what it meant.

The governor of Massachusetts at the time was John Leverett, who had been a Captain of Horse under Cromwell all through the great rebellion; and upon him and the Boston members of the council the conduct of the war now devolved.

The ill news had come on the 21st, and on the 26th two of the companies marched for Swansea, where the war had broken out. We get some idea of the character of the men from a little incident that befell them when they reached the Neponset River, at a point about twenty miles from Boston. At that moment there was a very complete eclipse of the moon; and some of the soldiers thought it of evil omen, and that the darkness on the disc looked like the figure of an Indian scout. Others, however, were reminded of what Crassus had said when the moon was eclipsed in Capricorn: "that he was much more afraid of Sagittarius than of Capricornus." Daniel Henchman, who had been a teacher in the Boston Latin School, commanded one of the two companies, and hence perhaps the classic remembrance, which is none the less a typical story. The army as a whole was in fact thoroughly representative of the people. The second generation had now grown up to do the fighting, while the older men who had led the people into the wilderness still formed the council and gave directions. The soldiers were fair examples of the community which they went forth to defend. The officers were the men of property and standing in the community, while the rank and file were the farmers, the mechanics, and the shopkeepers, well educated for those days, and deeply religious, but none the less able to march far and fight hard. They went to battle in discharge of their plain duty to Church and State, and they carried into the business of war the same grim determination and relentless thoroughness which they showed in all the affairs of life.

The little army reached Swansea by forced marches in forty-eight hours, and destroyed the village and wigwam of King Philip, as they called the leader of the Indians; but the great chief himself unluckily escaped. They then made a treaty with the Narragansett tribe, and soon after returned to Boston, while the war drifted away from the south to the towns on the more western frontier. Boston itself was too distant from the scene of war to suffer from a direct attack; but it was the centre from which troops went out, the spot where the forces were organized, and where all the conflicting rumours came. These rumours were generally terrible, but they were hardly worse than the truth. One village after another was surprised and burned; the men were slaughtered, and the women and children carried off into captivity. More than once the troops were caught in a deadly ambush, and "Bloody Brook" still retains in its name the memory of a fight where the "Flower of Essex," as the company was called, lost fifty-nine men.

To Boston also were brought the prisoners, and there many of the Indians whom the magistrates esteemed guilty were put to death on the gallows. The war assumed such proportions during the summer that the colonists soon found they were fighting for life. The powerful Narragansetts broke their treaty; a thousand men were raised on the first call for troops, and on the 13th of December, 1676, the colonists stormed the Narragansett fort, and after a severe loss took it, and finally broke the power of that formidable tribe. Thus the struggle rolled on, with massacres and ambuscades and much fierce fighting on the frontier, and with days of fasting and prayer, and much raising of men for the army in Boston. At last the colonists prevailed. On the 29th of June, 1677, there was a public thanksgiving for the victories; and on the 12th of August, Philip, the Wampanoag chief and the author of the war, was at last overtaken and slain.

With a population of about twenty-five thousand, Massachusetts had lost in battle during the war from five hundred to six hundred of her fighting-men of whom over one hundred, including four captains, were from Boston, and of the heavy taxation made necessary by the war, Boston had borne a third. It was in the midst of this struggle, when the colonists were fighting for life and for the preservation of English supremacy, that Randolph arrived to begin the second attack upon the charter. The time selected and the man chosen for the work were both characteristic of the Stuart government, a happy combination of mean heartlessness and treacherous intrigue. There was no ray of sympathy in Randolph for his countrymen engaged in a desperate war, but he was a good deal impressed by the appearance of their troops, of which he wrote,—

> Each troop [of horse] consists of sixty horse besides officers; and they are well mounted and completely armed with back, breast, and headpiece, buff-coat, sword, carbine, and pistols, each troop distinguished by their coats. The foot also are very well furnished with swords, muskets, and bandoleers. The late wars have hardened their infantry, made them good firemen, and taught them the ready use of their arms.

The Puritans of New England like their brethren in England were a fighting people, and were true to the traditions of Cromwell; but although this savage war had given them an

effective army, the loss of men and the burden of taxation had
weakened their capacity for resistance to the attacks of the Crown.

The times were unfortunately ripe for
such work as Randolph was set to do.
His first visit however was a short one.
He laid before the magistrates the
king's letter of March 10, 1676, and
copies of the complaints of Mason and
Gorges, informing them that an answer
must be sent in a month. Then after
prowling about among the New
Hampshire towns to gather up all the
complaints he could scrape together
against the Massachusetts government,
he sailed for England on the 30th of

With prompt shrewdness the colony bought up the rights to Maine for £1,200. The rights to New Hampshire they unfortunately were unable to buy.

July. The people held a meeting on the 9th of August, drew up a
brief declaration as to their rights, and sent Messrs. Stoughton and
Bulkeley as agents to England to plead their cause. When the
agents arrived they found that Randolph had been at work, and
that the minds of the persons in authority were already prejudiced
against them. The chief-justice declared that Massachusetts had no
claim to either Maine or New Hampshire, and that the grant of

Maine belonged to the heirs of Ferdinando Gorges. With prompt shrewdness the colony bought up the Gorges rights to Maine for £1,200; but although this bold step saved to them a vast territory, it prejudiced them more than ever in the eyes of the king. The rights to New Hampshire they unfortunately were unable to buy from Mason.

The ancient spirit which made the colony in its earliest and weakest days ready to face the power of England, and if beaten to retreat into the wilderness, had died down. Business prosperity had raised up a class of men who had accumulated property, and who therefore feared disorder, or anything which seemed likely to disturb the existing state of things. This party of timidity and moderation, although not strong in numbers, had weight in other ways, and was led not only by worthy persons like Bradstreet and Stoughton, but by schemers like Joseph Dudley, who saw prospects of personal advancement in loyalty to the Crown, and who were quite destitute of the fervid faith which had founded the settlement in the wilderness, and to which relenting or compromise was impossible. The great body of the people were true to the charter, and were ready for extreme measures; but although strong in numbers they were weaker than their opponents in position and wealth, as well as in the arts of political management. The result was that the struggle soon became an unequal one. On the one side was a determined enemy, pushing steadily forward toward a single object; on the other, a policy fluctuating between a general lack of energy and an occasional decided but often ill-advised resistance. Gradually, however, one point after another was yielded; and as the colonies fell back, the demands of the Crown advanced. The Puritans nevertheless although ready fighters were by no means bad negotiators. They understood fully the value of delay; and their clumsy rhetoric and long-drawn petitions and appeals which seemed to concede much and really gave up very little, were all well calculated to spin out the time and take advantage of the chapter of accidents which had favoured them so signally in the past.

Thus arguing, and yielding inch by inch, they managed to put off the dreaded fate for nearly nine years; but at last the blow fell. On June 18, 1684, the Court of Chancery made a decree vacating the charter, and giving the defendants till the next term to appear. They appeared accordingly at that term, and asked for time to appear to plead; but the Lord Keeper refused the motion, and finally judgment was entered. When the decree was known in Massachusetts in January, 1685, the General Court ordered a day of fasting and prayer, and made an address to the king; but all men felt that the old system had received its death-blow. The machine of government moved on mechanically for another year; and then while the last General Court elected under the charter was still in session, a frigate arrived bearing Randolph and a commission for the officers of a new provisional government, in which Joseph Dudley was to be President. The General Court made a reply to this commission, and then adjourned to the second Wednesday in October, never to meet again under the provisions of the old charter.

The State was harsh and intolerant in religious matters; but it threw open the doors of the schoolhouse to every child.

Under the government which thus came to an end in the summer of 1686, and which represented so much suffering, so much faith, and so much courage, Boston had grown from a scattered settlement on the edge of the wilderness to be a thriving and well-built town. At that time it contained about six thousand inhabitants, the houses were principally of wood, but many were of brick or stone, and in some instances the material had been brought from England. It was distinctly an English town. The migration had been an unmixed

one; and although the people had left their native country on
account of religious differences, they had brought with them all
their habits, customs, and modes of thought, which they had
inherited from their ancestors, and to which they were profoundly
attached. The names which they gave to their counties and towns
and even to the streets were English names, taken from well-
beloved places which they had left. They planted English fruits
and English flowers in their gardens, they filled their houses with
English furniture and built them in the style of English domestic
architecture; and yet, although in these ways they manifested their
attachment to the homes which they had left, in matters more
essential than houses and clothes and furniture they showed that
the spirit of a new country was upon them, and that they were
seeking to lay the foundation of a new nation among the people
of the earth.

The town of Boston was governed by the town meeting,
which has been compared with the "Folk-moot" of the early
English, where all the people met to consider the matters which
concerned the municipality. It was here that the lessons in self-
government were learned which prepared the way for the great
democracy destined to grow up from these feeble colonies. In the
same way the government of the State was one which the Puritans

had developed to suit their own theories. It was harsh and intolerant in religious matters; it was broad and liberal in the line of politics and popular education. It sent constables into the inns to stop men drinking; it punished those who failed in attending churches; it regulated what the men and women should wear; but it threw open the doors of the schoolhouse to every child, and even when hastening to its fall dared to tell Charles II. that it could not submit to the Navigation laws, because the colonies were not represented in the Parliament of the nation. Their legislation was severe, but the Puritans were never troubled if any one objected that their laws were sumptuary laws. They believed it to be the first duty of man to worship God and lead a moral life, and they thought that government was instituted to see that this was done.

The government thus formed and founded had its defects, but it was at least strong and successful. The Puritan State rose steadily from the day that Winthrop landed, without any of the checks which had marked the growth of the other American settlements, and showed a fixity of purpose which did not recognize defeat. The government partook in every way of the spirit of the men who established it, and its laws bore in every line the imprint of their stern will and rigid conviction. The

Puritan was not only deeply religious, but he was also effective in the affairs of this world. He prayed long and fervently, he fasted often, and humiliated himself before the Lord many days in the year; but at the same time he sowed and planted and reaped. He cleared the forests, defeated the savages, built ships, and pushed his farms and villages ever further and further into the wilderness. Of all this eager life, Boston was the centre; and when Increase Mather described the town, he enumerated as many trades flourishing there as could be found in any English city. The people lived well, according to the ideas of those days. All food supplies were cheap and plentiful, and game abounded. The dwellings were substantial; but their owners must have suffered severely from the cold in houses which had no appliances sufficient to cope with the rigours of a New England winter. The weak and sickly had but a slight chance for life, and the law of the survival of the fittest was terribly enforced by natural conditions. The only intellectual interest was found in religion, and in a creed of the most gloomy kind. On this they spent their mental energy with much solemn

The love of learning was kept alive by the clergy and the college, but the supply of books was meagre.

gratification to themselves and a good deal of discomfort to those who happened to differ from them. There were no amusements, and the literary movement which was soon to enter on a period of great activity had hardly got beyond an account of the country or the publication of a tract or occasional sermon. The love of learning was kept alive by the clergy and the college, and the people were educated and intelligent. But the supply of books was meagre, and the opportunities for reading or study, outside of religion and theology, were limited in the extreme. The people of Boston practically went from work to religion and from religion to work without anything to break the monotony, except trouble with England and wars with the savages. It was a simple, hard-working community, where there were no poor and few rich people. They were vigorous and self-reliant; they had prospered in worldly matters, and they had built up a goodly town; they had laid the foundation of popular education and democratic government; and they had tried under these conditions to make the Church and State one. Even when they had everything under absolute control, they had failed in their efforts to suppress freedom of religious belief. Now the charter, under which they had enjoyed power and exercised independence, was taken from them; and with sorrowful thoughts and many grievous forebodings the people of Boston entered on the second stage of their history, in which they were to be no longer a law unto themselves, but were to work out their theories and their destiny under new and widely different conditions.

Monument on Beacon Hill
(as it would be depicted c. 1811)

5. Under the Crown.

THE TEMPORARY government which took control after the loss of the charter was headed by Joseph Dudley, who had already begun to find his reward in adhering to the Crown, and who was managed and directed by Randolph. Beyond celebrating the birthdays of the king and queen, the new government marked its advent by only one important act,— they granted to Episcopalians the right to hold services in the east end of the Town House. At the same time, Judge Sewall—"Samuel Sewall the good and wise," the Puritan Pepys, as he has been called,—notes in his diary on the 5th of August,

> William Harrison is buried, which is the first I know of buried with the common prayer book in Boston.

On the 8th of August, he writes,

> Sabbath day. 'Tis s^d ye Sacramt. of ye Lord's Super is administered at ye Town. H. Cleverly there.

A month later he notes that

> David Jeffries and Betty Usher were married
> by the church service.

These were only forms and ceremonies, but they were
nevertheless the outward marks of a very vital change as well as
of the coming of an outside power, and they sank deeply into the
hearts of the colonists, who regarded them with grim dislike.
Dudley's presidency however was of short duration; for on the
19th of December, 1686, the frigate "Kingfisher" sailed into the
harbour, bringing the new governor, Sir Edmund Andros.

Andros was a gentleman of good family, and warmly attached
to the Stuarts. He had served in the army with distinction, had
married a lady of rank, and for three years had been governor of
New York. There he had ruled very successfully in the interests
of the Duke of York; and when James came to the throne, he very
naturally turned to Andros as a person well fitted, both by his
experience and his zealous personal loyalty, for the government
of the New England colonies. For many generations, so vigorous
is the life of political tradition, Andros has been held up in New
England history as a typical example of a cruel tyrant and a fit
representative of a bigoted and despotic master. There does not

seem to have been any better ground for this view than the bitter and natural hostility of a people who had been deprived of their independence, and whose religious prejudices had been wounded by the political change which he happened to represent. Andros was not only a man of good character and standing, but he seems to have been personally above reproach, and to have indulged in no petty oppression. The opposition to his government was perfectly sound, but it rested in reality on political and not on personal grounds. Andros was a good administrator, who served a stupid and oppressive king; and his policy, which was necessarily that of the Crown, was in consequence stupid and oppressive too, and could not have been better designed to raise a revolt in Massachusetts, if such had been its set purpose. The governor contrived by two acts to rouse against himself and his government every element of opposition among the colonists when it was perfectly possible for him to have divided instead of uniting them, and to have built up a strong body of supporters.

> *Andros was a good administrator, who served a stupid and oppressive king: his policy could not have been better designed to raise a revolt.*

The most distinguishing outward mark of the religious system of the Puritans was that they combined with an immense amount of religious devotion a total absence of outward ceremonial. When John Endicott cut the cross from the flag because it savoured of idolatry, he gave living expression to one of the most fervent beliefs of the Puritan heart. Forms and ceremonies, symbols and signs, were to them marks of the Beast. They attached to them a meaning and importance which it is hard for us in these days to realize; and they carried out their hatred of form to the last point. They prayed and preached at greater length and with more fervour than perhaps any people in the world; but they did it as the spirit moved, and not on the lines laid down by any man's mass-book or liturgy. During the years of their independence they had given full scope to their feelings in this respect. Their church government was democratic and independent, and their church services were stripped of all forms and decorations. They made marriage a purely civil contract, they wiped from their calendar all the church festivals and holidays; and when death came to a household, they took their dead from the home to the grave and laid them in the earth in silence. To such a people, wedded to such customs, it was a cruel shock to have a priest in a surplice conducting an English service in their Town House. To see men buried according to the prayerbook, and to behold marriages solemnized by the rites of the English Church, were sights which from their novelty may have interested the floating population of the little capital, who were undoubtedly entertained by the celebrations of royal anniversaries and by the re-appearance of old sports upon certain holidays. But if these things made the curious wonder, they made the judicious grieve.

Three years later an Episcopal church, the King's Chapel, was built on the spot where it still stands, but nothing could undo the effect of the seizure of the Old South Meeting and the performance there on each Sunday of the English service. By these acts Andros not only put an affront upon the clergy, the most powerful class in New England, but he alienated from his Government every Puritan, no matter how liberal or friendly or well inclined he might have been.

The other branch of his policy touched the people in a wholly different way, but on an equally sensitive point, for it menaced their property. In March, 1687, he and his council passed an act for levying taxes, and constituted the selectmen in every town and a commissioner, elected for the purpose, local tax commissioners, who were to furnish a schedule of persons and estates. This was received with much sullen opposition, which finally broke out in the town of Ipswich, where the people refused to pay the taxes because they were not levied by the General Assembly. These contumacious persons were tried on the 20th of October by a court composed of the governor's adherents, and were promptly convicted and fined. Not content with this, Andros, who does not seem to have been the person responsible for this scheme of taxation, went a step further, and advanced the theory that the Crown owned the fee to all the land, and that the existing owners must have their titles confirmed by the Crown. The friends of the new establishment obtained speedy confirmation of their titles on very easy terms, but it looked as if there was opened to the less pliant a wide prospect of extortion and loss of money. Thus Andros, by these two branches of his policy, drove into united resistance everybody who cared for the religion of their ancestors and every man who had property to lose. No better preparation could have been made for a successful revolution, and the outbreak was not long in coming.

Andros was frequently called away during his administration by the affairs of his extensive government, and also by the Indian troubles to the eastward. He returned from one of these expeditions in March, 1689; and soon after, on April 4, John Winslow arrived in Boston, bearing copies of the proclamation which had been issued by William of Orange on his landing in England. Not more than a spark was needed to fire the train prepared by the injudicious measures of the Andros Government; and this proclamation was a blazing torch, which of itself was enough to light the flames of insurrection. It had at once the important effect of rallying the upper classes and the old leaders to an open movement against the Government; but it is pretty evident that even this slight outside impulse was not needed among the people at large. They were ready to take their lives in their hands and defy all the power of England, rather than submit longer to a government which meant, as they had come to believe, the overthrow of their religion and the destruction of all their hard-earned property and dearly-bought rights.

At eight in the morning, it was reported at the South End that the people were in arms at the North End; and a like report was spread at the North End. Thereupon the people rose.

During the fortnight which followed the arrival of Winslow, Andros wrote that there was "a general buzzing among the people;" and on the 18th of April he found out what the buzzing meant. On that day, at eight in the morning, it was reported at the South End of Boston that the people were in arms at the North End; and a like report was spread at the North End respecting the South. Thereupon the people rose. They seized the captain of the British frigate, beat the drums, and set up an ensign on Beacon Hill. The old leaders of the popular party came forth and made their way to the Council House, where from the gallery they read William's declaration to the people; and in the mean time the immediate followers of Andros were seized and thrown into prison. The declaration read, they sent to Andros, announced that his authority was at an end, and demanded that he deliver himself up, which he refused to do. By two o'clock, however, not only the people of the town were in arms, but the soldiers from the country were pouring in in great numbers. Hearing that Andros was trying to escape to the frigate, they seized the boat and prevented his escape. They then surrounded the fort and again demanded his surrender. This time he gave way, and with his friends was marched to the Council House, and the next day was confined in the fort. The gentlemen who had taken charge of the movement immediately called a convention, at which it was held that the old government was in force, and Bradstreet and the council of 1686 thereupon returned to office. On May 26 they proclaimed William and Mary, and in December received orders to administer the government until otherwise directed. Orders also came to send Andros and his friends to England, whither they departed in February, 1690.

No more bloodless and effective revolution was ever carried out. It was the first forcible resistance by the people of Massachusetts to the Crown, which, after fifty years of independence, had stepped in and deprived them of their charter. But although it was the first, it was by no means the last; and the contest thus begun was continued in various forms until the colonies finally separated forever from the mother country. It was a very characteristic and law-abiding revolution, this rising against Andros, and shows not only the temper of the people but also their perfect union when the rights which they considered essential were attacked.

The colonists however had at an earlier date taken steps to seek relief in England, not anticipating such a speedy culmination of the conflict as actually occurred. In April, 1688, the Rev. Increase Mather had slipped away to England to represent before the king the cause of the people against Andros. He reached England in May, 1688, just when the seven bishops had signed the petition requesting the king to dispense with the reading and distribution of the declaration of indulgence, for which the people of New England not understanding its purport or policy had sent their loyal thanks.

Increase Mather was the ablest member of the most remarkable clerical family produced in colonial Massachusetts. He was a man of learning, with great force of will, determined and combative, and devoted to the interests of New England, as he understood them. He had much of the fighting Puritan in him, but also had qualities which were found in large measure among some of the elder Puritans, and which still occur among their descendants. Rigid as he was in defence of his beliefs, he was at the same time both astute and adroit, with a natural genius for diplomacy and politics. He was inclined on his arrival to accept the declaration of indulgence, upon which the English dissenters were divided; and he had an audience with the king, who gave him a gracious reception. After this favourable beginning he sought first to check the progress of Episcopacy, and then to settle the land-titles in Massachusetts. For this purpose he judiciously made friends among those who were near to James, with prudent toleration including among them such very different persons as William Penn, Lord Sunderland, Jeffries, and even Father Petre. He wrote also a pamphlet about New England, and had further interviews with the king; but although he received plenty of promises, he obtained nothing more, and his demands sank as his hopes failed. A great change however was at hand. In November, 1688, William was at Torbay; and in February, 1689, William and Mary were proclaimed. No one trimmed his sails more quickly to the fresh breeze than the shrewd New England minister. Mather made friends with the new sovereign as rapidly as with the old, and much more effectively. It looked at first as if he would be able to obtain the first charter; but the delays which ensued gave time for all the enemies of the old system to show themselves, and also for the arrival of Andros. Then Mather found himself involved in many bitter controversies, which he waged with great ability both with tongue and pen; but although the king continued to be favourable, he had no mind to set up an independent government in one of his provinces. Mather failed therefore to get the old

No one trimmed his sails more quickly to the fresh breeze than the shrewd New England minister.

charter, but he succeeded by quite a dexterous effort in separating New England from the other colonies; and he secured a new charter much more liberal than that granted to any other colony. He could not prevent the provision for a royal governor with a veto power; but he succeeded in annexing the territories of Nova Scotia, Maine, and Plymouth to Massachusetts, and in having all the grants made by the General Court confirmed. He also succeeded, when the charter had been signed, in practically picking out the governor. His choice fell upon Sir William Phipps; and thus equipped with his new charter and his new governor, Mather sailed for Massachusetts in March, 1692. Under all the circumstances, and considering the weakness of his position as the representative of a subject colony, it was a great triumph of diplomacy, in which subtlety and audacity mingled in nearly equal proportions. It was a fit forerunner of the triumph of that far greater New England diplomat, who nearly one hundred years later secured the alliance of France, and set his name to the treaty which forever separated England from her colonies.

A North East View of the Great Town of Boston

6. Under the Province Charter.

THE MAN whom Increase Mather brought with him to be the first in the line of royal governors of Massachusetts was more interesting personally, than as a statesman. Born in the woods of Maine, one of a family of twenty-six children, and left to pick up his living as best he might, William Phipps had worked his way up from being a shipwright and seaman, until a wild adventure gave him a fortune enormous for those days. He had come to Boston in 1673, worked at his trade there, and learned to read and write,—a new accomplishment to him, although he was then twenty-two years old. For some time he struggled along in comparative poverty, sailing on various ships, and taking part in expeditions against the Indians. On one of his voyages he heard of a Spanish treasure-ship which was sunk in the waters of the Spanish main. Thereupon he went to London, young and unknown as he was, in 1684, and managed to so plead his cause that James II. gave him an eighteen-gun ship and ninety-five men.

With this outfit he made a two years' cruise in the West Indies, but all he obtained was the knowledge of the precise spot where the treasure-ship had foundered nearly half a century before. He then returned to England for fresh aid, and managed to obtain another vessel, which was furnished him by the Duke of Albemarle and other courtiers, on shares. This time he succeeded. He found the sunken galleon, raised bullion from it to the value of £300,000, together with precious stones, and for his own share received £20,000, and was made a knight. He came back with Andros as high sheriff, an office in which he did not distinguish himself, as he knew nothing of law, and could not write plainly. He then made another voyage to England, came back again to Boston, where he built for his wife the "fair brick house" which he had promised her in the days of her poverty, and led a successful expedition against Acadia, where he took and plundered Port Royal and some other of the French settlements. He then undertook an expedition against Quebec, in which he failed disastrously. Again he returned to England, and again he came out, this time as governor. His administration, which was a short one,— lasting only two years and a half,—was more picturesque than important. He visited his old comrades the ship-carpenters, joined the church, to the edification of all good citizens, quarrelled with the other officers of the government, and wound up by knocking down the captain of a British frigate in the streets, and thrashing the royal collector of customs, with much consequent loss of dignity. The result of all these doings was that he was summoned to England in 1694, and died there a few months after his arrival, in February, 1695.

The most marked event of Phipps's administration was the outbreak of the famous witchcraft troubles, for which he constituted, with a fine neglect of legal niceties, a special court. There is no need in the history of Boston to enter into any detailed account of this hideous epidemic of superstition and panic which raged for months in the colony, and which is known to us as the witchcraft delusion. Prior to this, and at different times, two or three witches had been executed there in conformity with the brutal law and stolid superstition which then existed on the subject. About these early cases it is not necessary to say anything. They resembled hundreds of similar instances then occurring in

The most marked event of Phipps's administration was the outbreak of the famous witchcraft troubles, for which he constituted, with a fine neglect of legal niceties, a special court.

England. But not long before the great outbreak at Salem, there occurred in Boston the somewhat notorious affair of the Goodwin children, who were the special care of Cotton Mather, and whose case deserves fuller consideration than those which preceded it.

The best condensed account is that given by Governor Hutchinson in his history of Massachusetts, which is quoted by Mr. Poole in the Memorial History of Boston:—

> In 1687 or 1688 began a more alarming instance than any that had preceded it. Four of the children of John Goodwin, a grave man and good liver at the north part of Boston, were generally believed to be bewitched. I have often heard persons who were in the neighbourhood speak of the great consternation it occasioned. The children were all remarkable for ingenuity of temper, had been religiously educated, were thought to be without guile. The eldest was a girl of thirteen or fourteen years. She had charged a laundress with taking away some of the family linen. The mother of the laundress was one of the wild Irish, of bad character, and gave the girl harsh language; soon after which she fell into fits which were said to have something diabolical in them. One of her sisters and two brothers followed her example,

and, it is said, were tormented in the same part of their bodies at the same time, although kept in separate apartments and ignorant of one another's complaints... Sometimes they would be deaf, then dumb, then blind; and sometimes all these disorders together would come upon them. Their tongues would be drawn down their throats, then pulled out upon their chins. Their jaws, necks, shoulders, elbows, and all their joints would appear to be dislocated, and they would make the most piteous outcries of burnings, of being cut with knives, beat, etc., and the marks of wounds were afterwards to be seen. The ministers of Boston and Charlestown kept a day of fasting and prayer at the troubled house; after which the youngest child made no more complaints. The others persevered, and the magistrates then interposed, and the old woman was apprehended; but upon examination would neither confess nor deny, and appeared to be disordered in her senses. Upon the report of physicians that she was compos mentis, she was executed, declaring at her death the children should not be relieved.

This case derives its peculiar interest from Cotton Mather, who embalmed it among the countless books of which he was the author, and who engaged in many controversies over it, as he did over most things with which he was concerned. Cotton Mather was the son of Increase Mather, and in his way was quite as distinguished a man as his father. He is perhaps the most prolific writer that Massachusetts has ever produced, and his works, however small their literary merit, are of inestimable value to the student of history and character. He took a profound interest in the case of the Goodwin children, visited in prison the unfortunate woman Glover, who was condemned for bewitching them, and endeavoured by prayer and religious services to restore her victims to health. It being decided that the woman was *compos mentis* she was executed, as we have seen by the extract from Hutchinson. The children, after performing feats which much resembled those of modern spiritualism, finally returned to their natural state, grew up, professed religion, lived apparently sober and respectable lives, and so far as we know never made any confession of fraud in regard to their early experience. Mather in dealing with the case adopted a settled policy. He believed that the victims of witchcraft could be saved by prayer, and he was also of the opinion apparently that accusations should not be multiplied, but when made either by bewitched persons or by those accused of witchcraft should be so far as possible suppressed. He did not therefore reveal the confessions of the unhappy Glover woman, and the case of the Goodwin children had no further results. A short time afterwards, when the Salem epidemic was raging, a girl named Mercy Short, who lived in Boston, declared that she had been bewitched by one of the women in prison at Salem, and proceeded to go through the usual performances of bewitched persons. Mather adopted with her his remedy of prayer, and he did the same in the case of Margaret Rule, a few months later. In both instances his policy had at least the result of preventing further accusations by the bewitched girls, and the history of Boston was not marked by any further executions such as were then taking place in the neighbouring town. That Mather was both vain and superstitious cannot be doubted even if he had not had his controversy with Robert Calef to enlighten us upon that point. At the same time it must be admitted that however gross his superstition may have been, his practical policy in regard to the matter of witchcraft was a humane one, much more so than the attitude then generally held in regard to the delusion in all parts of the world, and that his superstitious belief in witchcraft and diabolism was common at that day to the great mass of civilized mankind, both educated and ignorant. But these Boston cases were sporadic, and the town was but little affected by the doings at Salem in the way of actual cases of witchcraft. Indeed, as the Salem epidemic spread and gathered in force, it met finally with its most serious check in Boston; for there it actually threatened the governor's wife, and the governor returning from an expedition to the eastward put a stop to proceedings which had begun to menace the well-being of the entire community.

The administration of Phipps, owing to the character of the man, was so peculiar that it can hardly be said to have been typical of the royal governors who succeeded him; and yet we can find in these years the general outlines of the policy and events which characterized the history of Boston and Massachusetts under the provincial charter. The principal interest of the colony was in the Indian wars, which beginning again after a brief respite following the death of Phipps, and drifting away to the north and east, raged along the frontiers for the next thirty years with little intermission. These Indian wars differed very much in character from those of earlier times. The Indians were now organized and led by the French, men who not only had military experience, and European training, but who were able to deal with the savages in a manner of which the English were quite incapable. Against the savages alone the early Puritans of New England had shown themselves to be perfectly effective; but against the savages led and organized by Frenchmen, the colonists of a later day found themselves at the beginning seriously overmatched. It was many years before they succeeded in developing a class of Indian fighters who were as hardy and crafty as the savages themselves, and not much less cruel. Phipps's career in respect to the Indians very much resembled the history of the succeeding years. Relying on the force of the colony, he struck the French a heavy blow, and captured one of their towns; he then failed in a larger expedition, which sought nothing less than the conquest of Canada, while in the mean time the outlying settlements were surprised, farmhouses were burned, men were murdered, and women and children were dragged off into captivity. It was a period of wars in Europe; and whenever William or Marlborough fought the French, the Indians fought the English colonies.

Joseph Dudley, who arrived in Boston with a commission as governor on the 11th of June, 1702, was by birth a Puritan of the Puritans. His father, Thomas Dudley, was one of the most conspicuous and noble figures among the leaders of the early immigration. He had alternated in the supreme office with Winthrop; and with the exception of Winthrop there was probably no man to whom the people looked up with more reverence and respect. The son of such a father inherited, therefore, the good-will of the people among whom he was born; and he came at an early age into public life and public trust. He came upon the field of politics at the time when the colony was entering on its last struggle for the preservation of its charter and its independence. He appears at first to have been of the popular party, but it is evident that he soon saw that for his purposes the popular was not the winning side. He early became, therefore, one of the leaders of the party of submission, and was sent out to represent the colony as one of its agents in England, when he went completely over, and from being one of the moderate and submissive party, became an active adherent of the Crown. For this he soon reaped his reward in being sent out as President of the provisional government, which preceded the coming of Andros, under whom he subsequently held high office, and with whom he was identified both in policy and in popular hatred. After the revolution which dethroned the Stuarts, and sent Andros a prisoner across the ocean, Dudley returned to England, where he speedily gained the favour of the new rulers, was made governor of the Isle of Wight, and was elected a member of

Parliament. One would think that all this would have gratified an ambitious man much more than anything which a struggling colony on the shores of New England could offer; but, as so often happens, Dudley's cherished desire was to be the first man in his own village rather than second at Rome. He remained in office for thirteen years, and finally died, in 1720, at his estate in West Roxbury.

It is safe to say that of all the representatives of the Crown who governed in New England there was no one so cordially hated by the people as Joseph Dudley, who not only represented that outside power which they so disliked, but who was regarded as one who had betrayed his race and his religion. That he was judged very harshly in the fervour of the day, we may well believe; but that he was an astute, intriguing, double-dealing man, cannot be doubted. It was not merely that he deserted the popular side and counselled submission to England, for many honest men did that in the last days of the colonial charter; but he very obviously sold himself, and not only submitted but went over to the opposite side, and made himself the most active agent of a policy which he knew to be unjust and hateful to the people who

Of all the representatives of the Crown there was no one so cordially hated as Joseph Dudley.

had looked up to him and his father as leaders. When Andros fell, Dudley was committed to jail lest the outraged people should set upon him; and he was then driven forth from his native land a prisoner, and in disgrace. Now he had come back to rule over it, and his rule was like himself. He was by no means a stupid man. On the contrary, he possessed marked abilities, and was a good administrator. In some respects he was clearly in the right, as in his controversy with the Mathers in relation to the college, in which the governor's policy made for liberality and progress; but he was as clearly unsuccessful in regard to the Indian wars, and was charged, on what seems to be very good ground, with illicit trading in arms and goods with the enemy. He entirely failed, of course, to get on with the representatives of the people. He made attempts, in accordance with his instructions, to induce them to rebuild the fort at Pemaquid, to give him a suitable official residence, and to settle upon him a proper salary. All these things the General Court refused. The first two were unimportant enough, the third

He made attempts to induce them to settle upon him a proper salary, the principle for which the colonies ultimately went to war.

involved the principle for which the colonies ultimately went to war. If the governor was to receive a settled salary during his term of office, or was to be paid from England, the representatives of the people who were taxed would have no longer any control over him. Dudley was the first of the royal governors to begin the fight in regard to this matter of salary. For some time he refused the money-grants; but as he could get nothing else he at last gave way, although he was so disliked that there was hardly any year when he received more than £600. He was constantly quarrelling with the House of Representatives, negatived everybody nominated by the House for the Council who was in the least obnoxious to him, and undertook to go a step further and put his veto upon the choice of Speaker, in which he was finally compelled to yield. Thus it went on during his whole administration, the ill-feeling deepening between the Assembly and the governor, who was unable to advance a step in his purposes. With the accession of George I., Dudley retired from public life; and the office that he had sought so eagerly and held so long could have been little more to him than a bitter memory of disappointment and defeat.

A year later, 4th of October, 1716, the new governor appointed by George I. arrived. This was Col. Samuel Shute; and although a more honest man than Dudley, he was quite as rigid in his defence of what he considered the royal prerogative. His whole administration was from beginning to end one long quarrel with the Assembly.

George II. on coming to the throne pensioned Shute, and appointed as his successor, William Burnett, son of the celebrated bishop, who reached Massachusetts from New Jersey in March, 1728, and died at the Province House in Boston, in September, 1729. He was welcomed with a great deal of pomp and parade, and with a large expenditure of money for the small treasury of those days; and then before the rejoicings had fairly subsided he entered upon a fierce contest over the salary question, which lasted until his death, and embittered his whole tenure of office. The General Court would fix no salary, and the governor would accept no temporary grant, although the representatives raised their offer as high as £3,000. This determination and honesty were not without their effect on public feeling, although of no avail in changing the policy of the House. Despite their stubborn conflict the people liked Burnett, for he was open and fair in his contest; and they could not but admire the spirit with which he carried it on. When he died, they buried him with great pomp, and five years afterward voted his children £3,000. Then after the lapse of a year there came a new governor, another native of the Province,

Jonathan Belcher, under whom the vexed salary question finally came to an end.

Belcher was of good Puritan stock, but, like Stoughton and Dudley, was one of those who had found his profit in an early submission to the new order of things. He was a polished, well-bred and well-educated man, and although devoid of Dudley's treacherous disposition, was capable of intrigue and much subtlety in political management. He knew his own people well, and undoubtedly felt that he could succeed where others had failed. His hope was not unreasonable, but his fate did not differ widely from that of his predecessors. The lesser points of controversy, as invariably happened, gradually sank away, leaving in lonely distinctness this particular issue, which involved the question of principle. Belcher tried to divide his opponents, and to win the Council to his side, in which he very largely succeeded; but the House stood firm, and after much refusal to grant salary on one side and to accept presents on the other, in 1735 the Duke of Newcastle sent the governor orders to accept the sum granted for a year, and afterward to take the most he could get. Thus on this point the popular cause had triumphed, and it was not until the same question came up in another form that the matter of the governor's salary became again a political issue in Massachusetts.

The interest of this long and apparently petty fight over a salary lies in the proof it gave of the keen instinct of the New England people for the question in which a vital principle was involved. If the governor had a fixed salary, or if he was paid by an outside power, his official responsibility to the tax-payers was at an end. The people of Massachusetts saw this perfectly. Whether the formula of the moment be that taxation without representation is tyranny, or that the chief executive magistrate must depend on the people for his pay, the principle is ever the same,—that the secret and safety of popular government is in the responsibility of the officers of government to the people. This principle the Puritans of Massachusetts established when they set up their independent government under the charter. They clung to it through all the years of provincial government, fighting for it with all the royal governors and never losing sight of their object, until at last it brought them to war with England, and finally to complete independence. If any one in England had taken the trouble to study and understand these Colonial questions, they would have noted the political sagacity and tenacity of purpose of these people, and would have seen that meddling and misgovernment applied to such material might have disastrous results.

Belcher's general administration, which lasted until 1741, was peaceable enough outside the salary question, and the town and province throve. He then was succeeded by William Shirley, who continued as governor through the next fifteen years. Shirley had the usual controversies with the Assembly, which were considerably modified by the disappearance of the salary question; but his career in this country extended over a much wider field than any that Massachusetts could afford. It was the period of one of the great wars with France, in which the men of Massachusetts achieved the most conspicuous success that fell to the British arms.

When Shirley returned to England, in 1756, he was succeeded by Thomas Pownall, who came out when the colony was labouring amidst the debts incurred during the war, and when a new war, destined to be of much wider extent, and have results much more far-reaching than the one just closed, was breaking upon it. During this war which was world-wide and which, under the guidance of William Pitt, resulted in the downfall of the French power in America, Massachusetts played a great part. At this time, as usual when in presence of an enemy, the colonists allowed their quarrels with the governor to slumber while all worked together for the success of the campaign,—a policy which was by no means common in the American colonies of that time. Fortunately for them and for the cause in which they were engaged, Pownall was the best of the royal governors. He was a wise and able man, who understood the people, and comprehended the prospects opening before the country. After his experience in America he went back to England to utter vain warnings in Parliament against the fatal policy which resulted in the division of the empire.

The line of the royal governors does not end with Pownall. There were two more to follow. But Pownall's administration, made honourable by his own career and brilliant by the successes of the war, closed the second period in the history of Massachusetts and of Boston. With the next governor, although the provincial charter still remained in existence, the colony entered upon the struggle with England in which it was to play the leading part, and which, after spreading to all the other colonies, culminated in the War of Independence. The first period in the history of Boston, covering the foundation and establishment of the Puritan settlements, lasted for fifty years, and was a period of complete political independence; then came the short despotic rule of Andros, the revolution which set William and Mary on the throne, and the entrance of the colony upon what may be called the second or Provincial period, under the provincial charter, and subject to the control of the mother country. The relations which the early Puritans had carefully severed were then renewed,—not only with England, but with all parts of the world. It was a period of great material growth, and throughout it all there runs the thread of continued resistance to outside government which the fifty years of early independence made natural if not inevitable. It was on the whole a quiet time and one of material prosperity, despite the continued Indian wars. The only question which really involved a fundamental principle was that of the governor's salary, and that was finally settled in favour of the representatives of the people of Massachusetts. In other respects the Ministry had wisely left the colony pretty much alone, and thus it came to the threshold of the most vital change in its history.

Faneuil Hall in 1775

7. The Capital of the Province.

THE CLOSE of what is known in our history as the Old French War, and the destruction of the power of France on the North American continent, marked a great epoch in the career of the English colonies. It was in fact the turning-point, where the colonies began to leave the colonial condition and to enter upon that of independent existence. This new movement was due to the removal of the power of France, which left the colonies entirely free to consider their relations with the mother country; for the dread of French aggression had been one of the strongest bonds between England and her colonies, and this bond was now destroyed. The mere fact that all danger from French invasion had been removed did not in itself mean that there was to be any revolution or any independence for the English colonies; but it none the less cleared the way for both these events, and made their coming easier. It was moreover the expense entailed by this war which brought upon the colonies the attention of England, with her consequent attempts at taxation, and thus began the great democratic movement that was destined to spread and grow far beyond the conception of any man then living, and to far outrun the limits of the continent where it started. With the end of the Old French War and the accession of George III., the period was reached in which Boston was to be the central point of the struggle then opening. Thus the town came quite without its own knowledge to the parting of the ways, and there is no point at which we can pause more fitly to look at colonial Boston than at the moment when she entered upon the movement which was to put an end to colonial existence.

It was the central point and chief city of the most compact population to be found on the Atlantic seaboard.

Boston had grown steadily, if not rapidly, in population since the days of Philip's War, when with some six thousand inhabitants it had contributed its large quota to the colonial forces, and borne the lion's share of the public expenditure. In 1760, Boston had about twenty-five thousand inhabitants, and was probably the largest, and was certainly the most important, town on the continent. This importance was not derived from the numbers of its people so much as from its foreign commerce, its trade and industry, the considerable amount of capital which was there accumulated, and from the fact that it was the central point and chief city of the most compact population to be found on the Atlantic seaboard. With the exception of London there were not many English towns which surpassed it in these respects, or were much ahead of it in population; and it was well known to the commercial world of England as one of the most important places in the British dominions. It still retained its English look; and Burnaby, who visited it about 1760, compares its appearance to that of a thriving English town. It had however greatly improved in outward appearance from the little Puritan town which had grown up under the old charter.

As seen from the harbour, Boston was formed of an amphitheatre of houses, rising gradually one above the other from the water's edge. There were many wharves built out with much industry; and conspicuous among them was the "Long Wharf," esteemed a prodigious work at the time, which was two thousand feet in length, and covered with handsome warehouses. From Long Wharf ran King Street, then the principal business street, through the heart of the town; and at its head was the Town-house, where the State Government in all its branches met, and beneath which the merchants held their exchange, and booksellers their stalls. The streets were sufficiently wide, but crooked and irregular, paved with cobble-stones, with gutters in the middle, and sidewalks marked off by a line of posts and chains. They were clean and well kept; and although not lighted with any sufficiency before the year 1773, were quiet and orderly. In the daytime the streets and squares swarmed with the eager life of a bustling, trading community; and there were many fine and well-stocked shops, as well as two fairs, one at each end of the town, which were held daily for ordinary traffic. To the south of the town there was a small but pleasant common, where, even at the end of the seventeenth century, John Dunton writes, that "gallants were wont to walk with their marmalet madams as we do in Moorfield."

There were also public buildings of no little pretence in size and appearance, and solidly built in the fashion of the eighteenth century. One of these was Faneuil Hall, which had been presented to the town by the rich merchant whose name it bore; another was the Town House, which still stands, like Faneuil Hall, practically unchanged; still another was the Province House, a handsome building where the royal governors lived and there were besides not far short of twenty churches, the majority belonging to the

Congregationalists, who were of course the prevailing sect. The harbour was always busy with shipping; and the Long Wharf, and its companions with their rows of warehouses, stretched far out into the water.

The changes in the appearance of the buildings and the streets were no less marked than those in the population itself. In the early days of the colonial charter, if there were few people who were rich, there were none who were very poor; but like all seaports, Boston soon gathered to itself a floating population, which formed a class unknown in the previous century. With the growth of wealth, differences in condition became more marked, and poverty ceased to be unknown. A workhouse and an almshouse were unpleasant evidences of the changes which had been wrought in this respect, and of the necessity which had arisen for public charity.

The increased number of school-houses showed that the Puritan policy of education had advanced with the prosperity of the community.

The increased number of school-houses showed that the Puritan policy of education had never been neglected, but had advanced with the prosperity of the community. The influence of the schools and the intelligent character of the population, were manifested also in other ways. There were now three or four newspapers, one almost as old as the century; and various attempts were made at periodical publications, with higher literary ambition than the news-letters and gazettes ventured upon. Book-stores too had increased, and the native publications had multiplied, indicating the presence of some literary activity, although its results are pretty well forgotten today.

In a similar fashion, although not so rapidly, the material interests and the amusements of the people as well had broadened and multiplied since the early Puritan days. Despite the kindly efforts of England to choke off American industries, manufactures were beginning to rear their heads; and ship-building occupied many persons, and brought much wealth to the Bay. In the methods of living, there had also been marked changes,—more marked of course in Boston than in the country towns, where there was no floating population, practically no mixture of races, and where the people clung to the ways of their ancestors with the stanch conservatism characteristic of their race. Much of the alteration in this direction was due to the political changes. The royal government brought with it not only a governor but a number of other Crown officers, who dressed handsomely and lived well, and whose scarlet coats stood out in bright relief against the sober Puritan dress, as did their dancing and merry-making against the sombre background of daily Puritan life.

The Puritans themselves, however, were not by any means averse to many of the comforts which money brings. Nearly forty years earlier, we learn from Sewall's Diary that one of his numerous courtships came to nothing, because he and the lady could not agree about keeping a coach; and we know from the valuations and the Acts of the legislature that there were many horses in Boston, and that coaches, chariots, chaises, and chairs were taxed, with the exception of those of the governor and the settled ministers. We can get the best idea on this point from the travels of Mr. Bennett, in 1740, whose observations are freely drawn upon by Mr. Scudder in his admirable account of life in Boston during the Provincial period. Mr. Bennett says,—

> There are several families in Boston that keep a coach and pair of horses, and some few drive with four horses; but for chaises and saddle-horses, considering the bulk of the place, they outdo London.

There were many handsome houses, some outside the town on fine country estates, but most of them within the city limits. Their owners suffered from cold, for the only method of heating was by wood-fires, and these were insufficient for the climate. "'T is dredful cold," writes Cotton Mather, in the year 1720, with his wonted simplicity of expression "my ink-glass in my standish is froze and splitt in my very stove. My ink in my pen suffers a congelation." With this important exception, however, the houses were probably as comfortable as any in the world, if not so splendid.

The furniture was English for the most part, and was both handsome and substantial. The houses stood generally in large gardens, and represented probably all the efforts of taste and luxury of which that day was capable. The men and women who lived in them, as we can see from Copley's pictures, dressed, despite their Puritan traditions, with all the richness of which silk and satin and lace were capable; while wigs, the coming of which Sewall had so exceedingly deplored, were universally worn in accordance with the last fashion in England.

The houses stood generally in large gardens, and represented all the luxury of which that day was capable.

Boston

The amusements of Boston were neither varied nor interesting, but still the people had amusements of a simple kind. Besides the universal athletic sports, and riding, hunting, fishing, shooting, and skating there were sleigh-rides in winter to some neighbouring tavern, followed by a supper and dance; and, in summer, excursions down the harbour, picnics on the islands, and little parties into the country to drink tea and drive home by moonlight. Theatres were strongly resisted, and do not seem to have been fairly established and accepted until after the Revolution.

Here is a contemporary account, much better than any which can be constructed now, of the way in which Boston people occupied themselves when not engaged in the serious affairs of business or religion.

> Every afternoon, after drinking tea, the gentlemen
> and ladies walk the Mall, and from thence adjourn
> to one another's houses to spend the evening,—those
> that are not disposed to attend the evening lectures;
> which they may do, if they please, six nights in
> seven the year round. What they call the Mall is a
> walk on a fine green common adjoining to the
> south-west side of the town. It is near half a mile
> over, with two rows of young trees planted opposite
> to each other, with a fine footway between, in

imitation of St. James Park; and part of the bay of
the sea which encircles the town, taking its course
along the northwest side of the Common,—by which
it is bounded on the one side, and by the country on
the other, forms a beautiful canal, in view of the
walk. Their rural diversions are chiefly shooting and
fishing. For the former, the woods afford them
plenty of game; and the rivers and ponds with
which this country abounds yield them great plenty,
as well as variety, of fine fish. The government
being in the hands of dissenters, they don't admit of
plays or music-houses; but, of late, they have set up
an assembly, to which some of the ladies resort. But
they are looked upon to be none of the nicest in
regard to their reputation; and it is thought it will
soon be suppressed, for it is much taken notice of
and exploded by the religious and sober part of the
people. But notwithstanding plays and such like
diversions do not obtain here, they don't seem to be
dispirited nor moped for want of them, for both the
ladies and gentlemen dress and appear as gay, in
common, as courtiers in England on a coronation or
birthday. And the ladies here visit, drink tea, and
indulge every little piece of gentility to the height of
the mode, and neglect the affairs of their families
with as good a grace as the finest ladies in London.

We get here a hint of what was undoubtedly the truth, that although the fine houses, handsome carriages, and rich dresses were shared by the more wealthy among the people of native stock, the amusements and modes of life which have just been described were confined almost entirely to the representatives of the Crown and their immediate circle. The great body of the population were still Puritans, liberalized and softened no doubt by the advance of time, but wedded to the traditions of their forefathers, and leading sober, hard-working lives. The mass of the population lived comfortably in good houses, gave their days to toil, and found their chief interest in religion; and although their mode of existence seems dull to us, it was probably of interest to them. They were the people who formed the strength and backbone of the Massachusetts community, and it was they who resisted England and fought out the War of the Revolution. Despite the outward changes among the upper classes,—for there was a very distinct aristocracy in Massachusetts as in the other colonies,—the Puritan ideas were too deeply branded to have been done away with by any change of government. We see proof of this in customs which look strange now, but which tell the story of the stern faith that had made the existence of the town and State possible. Sewall describes one custom which was exceedingly

characteristic, and if not picturesque, was at least interesting.
In the early days of the century, when the great curse of the
provincial trade was piracy, and when captured pirates were
brought to the town to receive their punishment, before they were
led to the scaffold they were always taken on a Sunday to one of
the churches, and there were preached at by the clergyman, to
the great edification of the congregation if not to that of the
criminals themselves. The Puritans were not a people who ever
shrank from the infliction of what they thought merited
punishment; and the penalties for crime in New England were
almost as severe and barbarous as in the mother country. But the
Puritan always prefixed to punishment the occasion which he
never lost for moralizing, even when the malefactor was not
condemned to death. If the offence was serious, the criminal was
taken about from church to church on Sunday after Sunday, and
used as a horrid example or text for the sermons of the divines,
and as a warning to the congregation.

Still deeper was the Puritan mark seen in the observance of
Sunday, which was planted so deeply among English-speaking
people that it remains to this day in its observances a monument
to the memory of the men who brought a king to the block, and
planted great commonwealths in the American wilderness. Let us

borrow again some of Mr. Bennett's words, which bring home to us more keenly than any modern description can, what a Sunday was like in the Boston of the eighteenth century:—

> On that day no man, woman, or child is permitted to go out of town on any pretence whatsoever; nor can any that are out of town come in on the Lord's Day. The town being situated on a peninsula, there is but one way out of it by land; which is over a narrow neck of land at the south end of the town, which is enclosed by a fortification, and the gates shut by way of prevention. There is a ferry, indeed, at the north end of the town; but care is taken by way of prevention there also. But if they could escape out of the town at either of these places, it would n't answer their end, for the same care is taken, all the country over, to prevent travelling on Sundays; and they are as diligent in detecting of offenders of this sort, all over the New England government, as we in England are in stopping up of highways,—more; and those who are of the Independent persuasion refrain any attempts of this kind, in point of conscience. And as they will by no means admit of trading on Sunday, so they are equally tenacious about preserving good order

in the town on the Lord's Day: and they will not suffer any one to walk down to the waterside, though some of the houses are adjoining to the several wharfs nor, even in the hottest days of summer, will they admit of any one to take the air on the Common, which lies contiguous to the town, as Moorfields does to Finsbury. And if two or three people, who meet one another in the street by accident, stand talking together, if they do not disperse immediately on the first notice, they are liable to fine and imprisonment; and I believe, whoever it be that incurs the penalties on this account, are sure to feel the weight of them. But that which is the most extraordinary is that they commence the Sabbath from the setting of the sun on the Saturday evening; and in conformity to that, all trade and business ceases, and every shop in the town is shut up: even a barber is finable for shaving after that time. Nor are any of the taverns permitted to entertain company; for in that case not only the house, but every person found therein, is finable.

As to their ministers, there is no compulsory tax upon the people for their support, but every one contributes according to their inclination or ability; and it is collected in the following

manner: every Sunday, in the afternoon, as soon
as the sermon is ended, and before the singing of
the last psalm, they have a vacant space of time,
on which there are three or four men come about
with long wooden boxes, which they present to
every pew for the reception of what every one is
pleased to put in them. The first time I saw this
method of collecting for the parson, it put me in
mind of the waiters at Sadler's Wells, who used
to collect their money just before the beginning of
the last act. But notwithstanding they thus
collect the money for the maintenance of the
clergy in general, yet they are not left to depend
entirely upon the uncertainty of what people shall
happen to give, but have a certain sum paid them
every Monday morning, whether so much
happens to be collected or not; and no one of them
has less than a hundred pounds sterling per
annum, which is a comfortable support in this
part of the world.

The English Church had broken in on many of the ancient
customs, with its ceremonials for weddings and funerals, and its
celebration of holidays, in a way which affected more or less the
whole population; but the religious character which the Puritans

had imprinted on their community could not be changed so soon by any example, or in so short a time as three quarters of a century.

Thus, then, the town comes before us as it stood on the verge of the most important years of its history, a vigorous,

Withal they formed a loyal part of the great British empire, and one which that empire could ill afford to lose.

prosperous, thriving town, stretching out its trade all over the world, building up its industry, gathering wealth, and growing in a steady, solid way, which gave good promise of strength and endurance. The people governed themselves in town meetings, and lived on the whole soberly and quietly after the fashion of their ancestors, educating their children, and sending one son when they could afford it to Harvard College, the height of Massachusetts ambition. They had long prayers and many sermons and lectures. There was but little light or colour in the dull life, except that which was given it by the Crown officers or by the strangers whom commerce brought within their gates. They were a sturdy people, too, very jealous of outside control, very watchful to see that their rights were not infringed, suspicious of all attempts on the part of the English Church to establish anything like Episcopacy, and yet withal they formed a loyal part of the great British empire, and one which that empire could ill afford to lose.

The Bloody Massacre perpetrated in King-Street Boston on March 5th, 1770 (Engraving by Paul Revere)

8. The Beginning of the Revolution.

IT IS said that almost all the family quarrels in the world grow out of some question of money, and this was certainly true of the great family quarrel between the two branches of the English race, which ended in the establishment of American independence. It grew out of differences as to the payment of money, but the principle which was involved finally was none the less vital; for it was the principle of free representative government which was at stake. Sir Robert Walpole, who was one of the greatest if not one of the purest and most virtuous of English statesmen, pursued toward the American colonies a policy of great wisdom. It is not clear whether he had laid down in his own mind and then carried out in practice any settled plan, but his attitude toward the colonies conformed exactly with his general theory as to what was best for England at that time. At home he aimed at peace and material prosperity, and strove by every means to gain time in order to enable the German dynasty to strike its roots so deep in the English soil that the old family could never come back. His policy toward America and her people was of the same character, but even simpler. He let them severely alone. The result was that the English colonies, not only in New England, where they had had a period of independent government, but all along the Atlantic seaboard, were strengthened on the whole in their attachment to the mother country. It was true that they wrangled with their governors and with the representatives of the Crown, but they found that in the long run they had pretty much their own way, and that in a war they had the vast power of England upon their side, and shared in the glory of an empire of which they were justly proud.

If succeeding ministers had inherited and carried out Sir Robert's policy, or had been great enough to understand the colonies as Pitt understood them, there might never have been a war for independence. There was nothing inevitable about the American Revolution. No long series of oppressions, as in France, had heaped up the explosive material which was certain sooner or later to ignite and produce a tremendous convulsion, both social and political. The people of the American colonies had not been oppressed, but on the whole had been very little meddled with, and in the main had been permitted to govern themselves pretty much as they pleased, which was equivalent, in their case, to having as little government as possible. Yet on the other hand, if there were no causes at work which were sure to bring about revolution at that particular time, the character of the people and their political habits were such that if they were once interfered with or oppressed, revolution was almost certain speedily to ensue. The standing grievances among the people of New England, and particularly of Massachusetts, were the Navigation Act of Charles II. and the Sugar Act of 1733. The New Englanders had shown always a fine disregard for these Acts of trade. They were violated in every direction, and public opinion, which is the foundation of all effective laws, not only did not uphold these statutes, but sustained the offenders against them. From a legal point of view these breaches of the laws were nothing less than smuggling, yet it was smuggling carried on to an enormous extent, not by individuals, but by States and communities. Now and then there would be a spasmodic attempt to punish infractions of the law, but on the whole these misdeeds, like everything else under Walpole that it was

If Bernard had been chosen with a view to his peculiar unsuitableness for the years which were to follow, no better choice could have been made.

inconvenient to deal with, had been let alone or winked at; so that the profitable, illicit trade had extended widely in all directions.

With the fall of Pitt and the coming into power of new men, who were only creatures of the young king, an era of experiment at once began; and improvements and reforms, as their authors considered them, were started everywhere throughout the government service. The Board of Trade, always inclined to be meddlesome, now thought it was high time to make the colonies auxiliary to English trade; and it was with instructions to this end that Francis Bernard came out as the successor of Pownall in the governorship. If Bernard had been chosen with a view to his peculiar unsuitableness for the years which were to follow, no better choice could have been made, a fact which was soon discovered. Bernard was not only bent on enforcing his instructions, but he was a narrow, captious man, utterly unable to understand the people, and gifted with a large capacity for making his policy disagreeable, without the strength necessary to carry it through, or to make himself or it respected.

For many years, in the relaxed condition of business under the Navigation Act, the custom-house officers, who according to the theory of the time came to the colonies chiefly for their own enrichment, had used their position to make their fortunes, probably by corrupt practices, and certainly by an abuse of the system of forfeitures under the Sugar Act of 1733. The methods of the custom-house officers and their exactions roused in time a great deal of feeling between them and the merchants and traders of the Province, both those who smuggled and those who carried on an honest commerce. At last, in the autumn of 1760, Charles Paxton, who was head of the Custom House at Boston, instructed one of his deputies in Salem to petition the Court for writs of assistance, which would enable the officers to forcibly enter dwelling-houses, stores, and warehouses in the execution of their duty, and for the purpose of seizing goods which they believed, whether rightly or wrongly, to be smuggled. This was a step beyond anything that had yet been done. The people were accustomed to chronic difficulties with the custom-house officers and were not at all sensitive to the ordinary procedure. But when it was proposed that these officers should be armed with a general, unlimited writ that enabled them at any time to enter the houses and shops, which the inhabitants of Massachusetts like all other English subjects believed to be their castles, there was added to the dread of unlawful exactions of money a keen apprehension that some of their most cherished principles were in danger. Resistance therefore to the application for the writs at once began, and a hearing was asked for by James Otis, who thus stepped upon the stage as the first, and one of the most brilliant, in the line of patriotic orators who did so much to argue the cause of the Revolution, and ultimately to bring on independence.

Otis was a young man of repute and standing, with a promise of great talents and of a prosperous future opening before him. He held at this time the post of advocate-general for the colony, but resigned it because he would not act for the Crown in this case and accepted a brief on the other side. The memorable hearing was held in February, 1761. Thomas Hutchinson, who had just succeeded Stephen Sewall as chief-justice, heard the case together with his four associates. The court sat in the council chamber of the old Boston Town House, a fine old room ornamented, as we are told, with two full-length pictures of Charles II. and James II., which unluckily have disappeared from human ken. The judges wore, after the fashion of the times, voluminous wigs and scarlet robes, and were a sufficiently imposing and dignified body. On this occasion the court-room was crowded, for it was well understood that this was a matter in which much was at stake.

For four hours he poured out a stream of eloquence. "Then and there," said John Adams, "the child independence was born."

The king's attorney argued the case for the Crown, and defended the validity of the writs on statute law and English practice. Oxenbridge Thatcher replied with a strong legal argument, taking the ground that the rule in English courts did not apply in America. If the case had stopped there, it would have been an interesting point in the development of the constitutional controversy then beginning between England and her colonies; but Otis, who followed Thatcher, gave the matter an entirely different turn. He went far outside any legal argument, and instead of the dry reasoning usually submitted to a court of the highest jurisdiction on a point of law, he made an impassioned speech, which took the question on to the broad ground of human rights. The echoes of that speech, of which only a few imperfect fragments survive in the notes of John Adams, have come down to us through more than a century vocal with many noises and much declaiming on all subjects. Otis said that the writs of assistance were instruments of slavery and villany, and that he appeared on behalf of British liberties. He declared that a man's house was his castle, and that this writ destroyed this sacred privilege; that its only authority rested on the law of the time of Charles II.; that no Act of Parliament could establish such a writ; and that it was against the principles of the British constitution. Thus for four hours he poured out a stream of eloquence, which did not convince the Court, who held the writs to be legal; but which roused the people, and filled their minds with thoughts of resistance to England. "Then and there," said John Adams, "the child independence was born."

As so often happens, however, the contest over the writs of assistance seemed at the time to be sporadic and isolated. We can see now that it was the first link in the chain of events which led to world-wide results; but at the moment the excitement died away, and nobody realized how deeply Otis's argument had sunk into the popular mind. This happens not infrequently with speeches which mark the beginning of a new era in politics. It was not until thirty years after the memorable day on which Webster made his famous reply to Hayne that men realized how that great speech had been silently educating the people of the United States in the arguments and beliefs which were to enable them to face and overcome secession. In the same way, it was little understood in 1761 that the words of Otis, and the dramatic occasion of their delivery, had filled the popular mind with ideas which were to come into active play years afterward, and produce the most far-reaching results. The legality or illegality of writs of assistance was a matter of small moment, but the eloquent argument which taught men to resent and resist outside interference was of the gravest consequence.

In England, certainly, the question of the writs of assistance and the arguments of a colonial lawyer made no impression. The new ministry went on in their appointed fashion. They were, as has been said, very anxious to enter on the path of improvement; but like many other reformers, they were especially interested in reforming somebody else. Charles Townshend, who was first Lord of Trade, and secretary of the colonies, had a complete scheme ready, by which he proposed to put aside not only charters and laws but the rights and privileges of the colonial legislature, and to grasp absolute power of taxation. This moderate and judicious policy did not immediately succeed; but not long after, George Grenville, in his capacity of first Lord of the Admiralty, thought that it was a good plan to have the naval officers act as custom-house officers on the American coast, and the bill embodying this idea became a law. Then Grenville became minister himself, with larger powers than ever, and proceeded to carry out still further his theory that the colonies should help to bear the

The legality or illegality of writs of assistance was a matter of small moment, but the eloquent argument which taught men to resent and resist outside interference was of the gravest consequence.

expenses of the British Crown. Grenville was a worthy person, industrious in business, of no slight ability, but wholly destitute of imagination, and utterly unable to appreciate the conditions of the colonies with which he was so ready to meddle. He therefore began while he was planning a colonial stamp act which was to pay the expenses of the army with a bill to impose duties on foreign commodities imported into America and on colonial products exported therefrom, together with a heavy duty on molasses and sugar, which formed the principal articles of trade in New England. This bill carried with it increased power for the Admiralty Courts, which was of itself deeply unpopular with the colonies, while the tax on sugar at once awoke the spirit of resistance. Otis came out with a pamphlet, an attempt was made to correspond with the other colonies, which was a most dangerous symptom, if England had had the wisdom to appreciate it, and the legislature addressed the House of Commons against the Sugar Act.

These acts however were soon forgotten in the one which followed in the next year, 1765. Then it was that Grenville brought in the famous Stamp Act, and passed it through the House,—not without some eloquent opposition, but still with no real difficulty. His lack of imagination had made him unable to anticipate in the slightest degree the effect of this legislation in America, but he had not long to wait in order to find out the view taken of his legislation by those against whom it was directed. The news of the passage of the Stamp Act lit up the flame of resistance to England from one end of the colonies to the other. It required no elaborate explanation to teach a people more keenly alive to their political rights than any in the world, that an act which proposed to give the power of internal taxation to a Parliament where they had no voice, required little addition to become as perfect a system of irresponsible tyranny as could be devised. It was not the taxation of the Stamp Act that alarmed them, but the principle involved in it. In Boston, feeling ran higher perhaps than anywhere else; and unfortunately it found vent not only in the measured and effective opposition of the leaders and of the great mass of the people, but in outbreaks of mob violence. The stamp distributor was hung in effigy, taken down in the evening and burned on Fort Hill, while the crowds in the streets were so violent and excited that Bernard and Hutchinson fled to the Castle. Rewards were offered for the apprehension of the offenders, but no one would act as informer. A few days later another mob gathered, burned the papers of the Register of the Admiralty Court, plundered the house of the Comptroller of Customs, and then sacked the house of Hutchinson, and destroyed his really fine library, a disgraceful and outrageous performance which did much to injure the great cause in which all the people were engaged. A public meeting the next day denounced this riot and its excesses; but despite this hostility to violence of any sort, the lawful opposition went on more vigorously than ever, and was much more serious than the outbreaks of the mob.

The legislature of Massachusetts passed a series of resolves declaring and setting forth the rights of the people, and this declaration of principles was circulated throughout America. Yet another resolve of the legislature, passed much earlier, bore fruit on the 7th of October, in the first American Congress, which met at New York, and which was composed of delegates from the different colonies. The Congress did nothing very formidable. In a very temperate way they expressed their views in their resolutions protesting against the extension of the admiralty jurisdiction and the imposition of taxes, except by their own representatives. To this they joined an address to the king, a memorial to the House of Lords, and a petition to the House of Commons. Their resolutions and addresses were however little more than an extension of what the separate colonial assemblies had already done. The great fact about these gentlemen gathered in New York was that they formed a Congress, because that meant a union of the colonies; and a union of the colonies was the one thing more fatal than any other to British supremacy.

When the 1st of November came, the date at which the Stamp Act was to go into force, there was in Boston a universal refusal to use the stamps. The bells were tolled, minute guns were fired, flags were hung at half mast, and the crowd gratified itself by hanging Grenville in effigy. His stamps, however, were required for every transaction, and business therefore came to a standstill at once. The ports were closed, vessels could not sail, business was suspended, and at the same time agreements were made by the people against using foreign importations. A month later efforts were made to open the ports and the Custom House, which were in a measure successful; but meantime the news of the outbreak of resistance in America travelling back to England had not only surprised but much alarmed the home Government.

In the interval which had occurred since the passage of the act, Grenville had fallen from power, the Rockingham Whigs had come in, and the political situation so far as America was concerned had radically changed. When Parliament reassembled, Pitt made his great attack upon the Stamp Act, in which he declared that he rejoiced that America had resisted. The assault was followed up, and on the 24th of February the House passed a bill to repeal the obnoxious law, which on the 17th of March received the sanction of the king. The news of the repeal was received in the colonies with the greatest joy. Every form and demonstration of pleasure was indulged in, and statues and pictures were liberally voted in all parts of the continent to Pitt and to the other friends of America in the House of Commons. The people, indeed, were so overjoyed that they did not notice that the English ministry in repealing the Stamp Act had made the fatal blunder of joining to it a declaratory act, in which they asserted that Parliament had the power to legislate for America in all cases whatsoever, thus reiterating the principle, which was the real thing at stake, while they gave up the practice, which was a merely temporary concession.

They had obtained the repeal of a particular law, but they had not obtained any concession of the principle of the law.

In a very short time the inevitable consequence of this declarative principle was seen in the passage of Townshend's Bill to levy duty on glass, paper, painters' colours and tea, and in the establishment of a Board of Customs at Boston, to collect the American revenue, which was to be at the disposition of the king for the purpose of supporting the officers of the Crown independently of the legislatures. The people of America now saw plainly that the victory over the Stamp Act, which had caused them such rejoicing, was in fact no real victory at all. They had obtained the repeal of a particular law, but they had not obtained any concession of the principle of the law. The repeal of the Stamp Act, followed by the declaratory act and Townshend's Bill, were in fact the first of a series of blunders with which, by infinite stupidity, the British ministry drove into rebellion a people whom they easily might have retained as loyal subjects of the British Crown simply by abstaining from oppressing them and by respecting their prejudices and habits of government.

"Like master, like man." The representatives of the Crown were reproductions in little of the ministers. Governor Bernard, who had a genius for producing useless irritation, refused to call the legislature, and thus brought into play on the largest stage that body which was destined to lead the way in the Revolution, the Boston Town Meeting under the lead of Samuel Adams. There, in town meeting, the people agreed not to import or use certain articles of British production, and there also they appointed a committee to extend their agreements and circulate their resolutions. When the Massachusetts legislature finally came together, in January, 1768, they too carried on the war again in the town-meeting fashion; and a circular-letter which they sent out, drafted by Samuel Adams, alarmed the Crown officers, and drew down the denunciation of the secretary of the colonies.

By the close of the year 1768, ships-of-war were in the harbour, and two regiments were landed, and encamped on the Common. The question was drawing very near to the point where something more vigorous than arguments about taxation would be needed to solve them. A year elapsed without a legislature; and when it was again convened, it proved to be no more pliable than its predecessor. The representatives refused all the governor's requests, and when at last he informed them he was going to England to lay the state of affairs before the king, the Assembly responded by a unanimous petition to the king to remove him.

On the departure of Bernard, Lieutenant-Governor Hutchinson came to the chair. He was a native of the Province, of old Puritan stock, a man of ability, and a capable administrator, who had filled many offices, and on the whole had filled them well. In peaceable times he would have left an honoured if not a brilliant name. Unluckily, he fell on a period when it was perhaps impossible for any representative of the Crown to succeed as governor of Massachusetts. Nevertheless, after making all allowances, and after freely conceding that it was his duty to be loyal to the Crown and to seek by every method to properly enforce the laws, there can be no doubt that Hutchinson failed completely in the task presented to him. Unlike his predecessor, he understood the people, and he ought to have known that the domineering methods of Bernard and the policy of the home Government were not only wrong, but were almost certain to hurry forward the very results which he most deplored. It was, perhaps, too late for any man to have affected the course of events, but it was certainly Hutchinson's duty, understanding as he did the Province and its people, to have pointed out to the ministry the proper course for them to pursue. He at least should have advised a return to the wiser system of Walpole. Instead of that he not only sustained the existing policy and urged its extension, but he secretly misrepresented the people to the home Government, and drove on the movements which he must have known in the end could result only in open war.

While the non-importation agreements were being carried out throughout the colonies with such success as seriously to injure London merchants and English commerce, the troops remained in Boston, and their presence was a source of continual irritation which nothing but their withdrawal could relieve. There were quarrels in the streets between the soldiers and the citizens, sometimes between individuals, and sometimes between groups on either side. The town was restless and uneasy under a presence which it hated, and the troops were defiant and suspicious. At last on the 5th of March, 1770, the fatal outbreak came. It was a moonlight evening, with a slight fall of snow glistening on the ground. During the afternoon there had been various trifling collisions between straggling soldiers and men and boys who were in the streets, brawls to which the town had become only too well accustomed. Then a little later came a brief struggle between some soldiers and some of the townspeople near the head of what is now State Street, which looked down toward the harbour and the shipping, over the Long Wharf, of which Boston commerce was so proud. The soldiers threatened to fire, and matters looked very serious, when an officer ordered the men into the yard of the barracks and had the gates shut. Unfortunately, the alarm bell already had been rung, and the people began to pour out into the streets, supposing there was a fire. When they found the occasion of the ringing, they scattered through the streets crying out against the soldiers, and making a good deal of noise and disturbance.

Not long after nine o'clock some of the townspeople approached the Custom House on the north side of what is now State Street, where a sentinel was posted. Voices in the crowd cried, "Kill him! Knock him down!" and the sentry threatened to fire. "If you fire, you must die for it!" called out Henry Knox, afterward Washington's Secretary of War, who happened to be passing. "I don't care," replied the sentry; "if they touch me, I will fire." Thereupon, the man levelled his gun, warned the crowd to keep off, and called to the main guard for help. In response to the cry for aid a sergeant with a file of men came from the Town House, and joined the sentry, together with Captain Preston of the 29th regiment. The crowd as they saw the soldiers loading began to shout at them, and dared them to fire. The excitement was rising fast, and the few men who kept their heads saw that great danger was at hand. Knox seized Preston and begged him to take his men back, telling him that if they fired, his life must answer for the consequences. The soldiers then began to use their bayonets, and the people to throw stones. There was great confusion and then decisive action. No one knew exactly how it happened, or who gave the order, but in a moment the soldiers fired point blank upon the crowd. Three men were killed by the volley and eight others wounded, two of them mortally. The people fell back at first, and then returned. Meantime, Captain Preston withdrew his men to the main guard; the drums beat to arms, and the 29th regiment began to form near the Town House. Now the alarm rang out everywhere in deadly earnest, and the excited people poured forth into the streets. It looked for a time as if war actually had come, with street-fighting of a bloody and disastrous kind. Fortunately, however, although the troops and their leaders showed a lamentable lack of steadiness and intelligence, the people were well led; and Hutchinson, who soon appeared, after questioning Preston, spoke to the crowd from the balcony, and declared that the law should have its course. The people, however, refused to disperse until Captain Preston was arrested. Thereupon a Court of Inquiry was held; Preston was bound over for trial, and the soldiers who had fired were placed under arrest.

It has been the fashion of late years to speak of what our ancestors called the "Boston Massacre," as a street riot, participated in by a disorderly class of people, and as something of which it was not desirable to keep alive the memory, or to be very proud. It is true that it was the outbreak of a town mob, and that the persons engaged in it belonged for the most part to the lower class in the community; although there was none of the criminal element from which the mobs of great cities are usually recruited, for Boston at that time did not possess a population of that character. It may be freely admitted also that the people upon whom Preston and his men fired were a street crowd, and that the outbreak was a disorderly riot. These facts do not in the least diminish the importance of the event itself. The fall of the Bastille was the work of a mob; a savage, ignorant, bloodthirsty mob, revenging past wrongs which made their own doings seem gentle and respectable. Yet the fall of the Bastille marked the beginning of the French Revolution, which shook the civilized world from one end to the other and wrought finally vast good to mankind. The instruments may have been rude, or even brutal, but their work was none the less momentous. In the same way, the Boston Massacre marked the beginning of the American Revolution, and the impulse which led to it was right, however faulty the means or the methods. The instinct of the people of Boston was against the presence of the soldiers quartered upon them, and their instinct was perfectly correct. The troops were the visible force, sent there from outside to sustain laws which the people believed fatal to their liberties; and the blind rage which led to the quarrel between the soldiers and the townspeople, as well as the final firing on the crowd, sprang from the instinctive conviction that the presence of these troops meant the overthrow of the freedom which the people most cherished, and which they had always possessed.

The instinct of the people of Boston was against the presence of the soldiers quartered upon them, and their instinct was perfectly correct.

The rioting and bloodshed were soon over, but not so their results. The next day a great meeting was held in Faneuil Hall;

and a committee of fifteen, headed by Samuel Adams, was appointed to inform the governor that the inhabitants of Boston and the British soldiers could no longer live together in peace or safety. In the afternoon the regular town meeting met to hear the report of the committee, who announced that they could obtain the removal of only one regiment. "Both regiments or none!" was the shout which went up from the people; and the committee went back again to see the frightened governor. The scene which then ensued is one of the dramatic scenes of the American Revolution. In the waning light, for the day was drawing to its close, Adams stood before

> *The people gave the protection of the law to the men who had wronged them, and thus asserted the predominance of the civil power.*

Hutchinson and argued the cause of the people. The governor resisted and temporized, retreated and advanced; but at last he gave way altogether, and both regiments were ordered out of the town and into the fort, to be known thereafter as "Sam. Adams' regiments." Owing to the abiding sense of law and justice, which was one of the strongest features of the New England people, Captain Preston and the soldiers had a fair trial, and were defended by John Adams and Josiah Quincy, two distinguished patriots. Six of the soldiers, together with the captain, were acquitted; the two men who were found guilty were branded on the hand. The punishment was as moderate as the trial had been fair and the verdict tolerant. But while the people of Boston and Massachusetts gave the protection of the law to the men who had wronged them, and thus asserted the predominance of the civil power, they buried their dead with a great funeral procession, on the 8th of March, and celebrated the 5th of March the day of the massacre every year thereafter until the 4th of July came to take its place. A people who could show as much self-restraint as was shown by the people of Boston after the riot and bloodshed of that March evening, were far more to be dreaded than if they had rushed forward in the path then marked out, and precipitated a civil war which had no better origin than a street-fight.

This may Certify all whom it may Concern, that the Bearer hereof
is an Inlisted MONTROSs at his
MAJESTY'S NORTH-BATTERY, in Boston under my Command.
Given under my Hand this   In the
Year of his Majesty's reign

1762 View of Boston Harbor
Showing Christ Church
(Engraving by Paul Revere)

9. Revolution.

BEFORE THE Boston Massacre had been heard of in England, indeed, upon the very day on which it occurred, it seemed as if a faint glimmering had come upon the king and his advisers that the course they were pursuing was not the very wisest in the world, and had not thus far been productive of much that was valuable, either to themselves or to the British empire. On the 5th of March, the day so memorable in Boston, Lord North brought in a bill to repeal the Revenue Act, with the exception of the preamble and the duty on tea. There was a suggestion of sense in this proposition, and yet all the British measures of conciliation led to the final separation of the colonies from the mother country, almost as much as the oppressive laws. They were marked invariably by one of two characteristics, or by both; they either came too late or they did not go far enough to do any real good, making some little reservation which destroyed their efficacy. Lord North's repeal of the Revenue Act belonged to the latter class. Like the repeal of the Stamp Act, it was either not worth doing at all, or else it should have been done completely. To reserve the principle, and to retain the duty on one article in order to demonstrate the right of Parliament to tax, was just as bad as to retain the duties on twenty articles and give up nothing. The colonies were fighting for a principle, not for relief from imposts; and this fact which was the key to the whole situation, the British ministry, gifted with a stupidity which seems now beyond nature, and attributable only to art, never could understand.

At the same time, however, the people of the various colonies, who were naturally loyal and by no means anxious to have a breach with the mother country, and who were desirous, after the fashion of mankind, to go on peaceably in their accustomed way, were quite ready to see in this partial surrender the promise of complete harmony in the future. Non-importation agreements relaxed in most of the colonies, and trade revived. Even in Massachusetts the movement in opposition to the Crown seemed to subside; but the town of Boston, which had already come into conflict with the home Government, was more on the watch than any other place in North America. In the progress of these events it had become the most conspicuous place on the continent. It had already engaged the attention, not only of people in England, but of shrewd observers on the other side of the Channel; and it was destined in a very short time to fix the attention of the civilized world. It looked like a terribly unequal conflict for the little town, determined as it was to enter upon such a contest, but it was leading in a great struggle for popular rights; and whether the people of Boston were conscious of it or not, they must have felt that in the end their cause would be that of every American colony.

In September, 1770, Hutchinson received a royal order which commanded him to give up the Castle to the English troops. This he did; and the Provincial Assembly solemnly protested against it as another and added grievance. At the same time they performed a much more important act than that of entering any protest, no matter how energetic, by selecting Benjamin Franklin to act as the agent of Massachusetts in England; and thus put forward the ablest man in America to present the cause of the colonies to England and to the world.

They performed a much more important act than that of entering any protest, by selecting Benjamin Franklin to act as the agent of Massachusetts in England.

The year following passed quietly. Hutchinson was at last commissioned as governor, thus attaining to the height of his ambition, and kept up more or less controversy with the legislature, of no very great meaning or importance now. These minor controversies indeed soon dropped out of sight when it was known that the governor had accepted a salary from the king in violation of the charter, and by so doing had made himself independent of the people. The House passed a vote of censure upon the governor's action, although they were unable to ward off the blow. But popular wrath was inflamed still more when it became known that the judges as well were to be paid from the royal treasury, and that thus justice also was to be independent of the people for whose use the Court was established. Then the town meeting of Boston took the matter in hand. They asked the governor to inform them as to the truth of this report about the judges, and then they petitioned him to convene the Assembly. When this petition was rejected, they voted the reply not satisfactory; and then at the same town meeting, where they resolved in favour of the right of petition, Samuel Adams stood up and moved that a Committee of Correspondence be appointed to state the rights of the colonies, and to communicate and publish the same to the several towns. Thus came the movement for union, which was a thing above all others to be

The movement for union began where it ought to have begun, in a New England town meeting.

dreaded by England. It began, where logically and scientifically speaking it ought to have begun, in a New England town meeting; and its first effort was toward uniting the other New England towns, which by their independent local governments were peculiarly fitted for political combinations. The towns responded, and the arguments of the committee spread beyond the limits which had been proposed, as undoubtedly was the intention of their framers, and were received eagerly in all the other colonies. The movement toward an American union was fairly on foot.

Even yet, however, the final conflict might have been long delayed had it not been for the duty on tea, which had been left by the wise ministry simply as an emblem of Parliamentary sovereignty. It is a risky business to erect monuments in the form of laws; for one can never tell when a law which is meant to remain merely as an expression of opinion, may be put into active operation. Such was now found to be the case. Early in the year 1773, the East India Company discovered that the American non-importation agreements had had the melancholy effect of obliging them to accumulate their teas in England, and they found themselves thus confronted with the prospect of no market and heavy losses. They therefore pushed an Act through Parliament authorizing them to export their teas without paying duty in England, which would enable them as they believed to sell the teas so cheaply in America that the colonies could not withstand the temptation, since the reduction would more than make up for the tax imposed by the Revenue Act. The company accordingly despatched tea-ships to Charleston, Philadelphia, New York, and Boston, with cargoes consigned to merchants in those cities. This was another piece of stupidity. Why the British ministers should have imagined for a moment that the Americans would not perceive at once that this was an attempt to make them pay the duty and concede the principle for which they had been contending, it is difficult to understand. If they laboured under any such delusion they were very soon to find out their mistake. The town of Boston, at all events, was resolved that there should be no misapprehension as to the cargoes shipped to that port. A popular meeting first demanded that the consignees should resign, which was refused. Then a town meeting was held on the 5th of November, at which John Hancock presided, and resolves were passed like those which had been adopted in Philadelphia. The consignees also were again asked to resign, and again refused. About a fortnight later news came that the tea-ships might be expected at any moment, and on the 18th of November another town meeting was held; once more the consignees were asked to resign, and once more they refused. Thereupon the meeting dissolved without taking any action, without passing any vote, and without expressing any further opinion,—an ominous silence which seems to have been more impressive to the consignees than anything else.

When the ship "Dartmouth" arrived on Sunday, the 28th of November, the Committee of Correspondence and the people were quite prepared for the crisis which was upon them. The Puritans and their descendants were very rigid in their observance of Sunday, but even their religious scruples gave way to political necessities. The Committee of Correspondence obtained a promise from Rotch, the owner of the "Dartmouth," that it should not be entered until Tuesday; and the towns about Boston were invited to attend a mass-meeting in Faneuil Hall the next day. So many men came in answer to the call that the meeting was obliged to adjourn to the Old South Church, where it was resolved that the tea should be sent back, and that no duty should be paid. At the adjourned meeting in the afternoon Mr. Rotch protested, but was told that if he entered the tea he would do so at his peril; and a watch of twenty-five persons was appointed to guard the ship. On Tuesday the consignees declared that they had not the power to send the tea back, but were ready to store it. Thereupon the governor issued a proclamation warning the meeting to disperse, which was treated with entire contempt. Then the consignees and the captain agreed that the tea should be returned, an agreement to which the owners of the other ships also gave their consent. Soon after the two other ships appeared, and were anchored near the "Dartmouth," so that they could all be guarded together. The ships could not be cleared from Boston with the tea on board, nor could they be entered in England. The people wanted to have the ships returned peaceably, and the consignees were now quite willing to yield; but Hutchinson would not give a permit, and the soldiers in the Castle prepared to resist their passage. The time at which the tea would be seized under the law and brought on shore was fast drawing near, but the last day was reached and the Collector of Customs still refused absolutely to grant a clearance to the ships, unless the teas were discharged. This was Thursday, the 16th of December. The Old South Church was crowded with

Samuel Adams arose and said, "This meeting can do nothing more to save the country." The words were of course a signal.

people, and Rotch appeared and reported that a clearance had
been refused to him. He was then asked to go once more to the
governor, which he did; and while he was gone the crowd
increased until by the afternoon over seven thousand people were
gathered in and about the church. The short winter day was
drawing to a close, and the dimly lighted church grew darker and
darker, while the people waited, determined to know the end. At
last Rotch appeared again, and reported that the governor would
not give a pass. The moment he had concluded his report Samuel
Adams arose and said, "This meeting can do nothing more to save
the country." The words were of course a signal. A shout was
heard in the street, and some forty or fifty men disguised as
Indians rushed by the door and down toward the wharves,
followed by the people. The "Mohawks," as they were called,
rushed on board the tea-ships and threw the chests of tea into the
bay. No violence was committed, and no tea was taken; the
cargoes were simply destroyed so that they could never be landed.
It was a picturesque refusal on the part of the people of Boston to
pay the tax. It was also something more. It was the sudden
appearance, in a world tired of existing systems of government, of
the power of the people in action. The expression may have been
rude, and the immediate result trivial, but the act was none the
less of the gravest consequence. It was the small beginning of the

great democratic movement which has gone forward ever since, and which it would have been well for English statesmen who were then concerned with it to have pondered deeply.

The Boston people well knew what their act meant; for this was not the doing of a riotous street-mob, but of the whole body of the citizens, led by their ablest men. It was a defiance to the British government. That act performed, only two things were possible: the British Crown was obliged either to yield and confess itself defeated, or to carry out its laws by suppressing colonial liberty with all the force at its command. No man who understood the situation could doubt for a moment what that choice would be, nor can we wonder that the British ministry determined to resort to force. It was through their blundering that such a situation had been created; but, as the situation actually existed, it was hardly to be expected that they, representing as they did the power of Great Britain, would meekly yield to the resistance of a single colonial town.

The news of the destruction of the tea aroused a deep interest in England, and the ministry at once set about meeting the issue which they had thus forced into existence. That they should undertake to vindicate the power of the Crown and uphold the laws was, from their point of view, wholly natural; but they went about their work with the stupidity which characterized them at

every stage of the American Revolution. Not content to take
suitable measures to enforce the laws, they set aside all laws, all
precedents, and every constitutional tradition; and without waiting
to investigate the case, or hear what could be said in defence, they
brought in the Boston Port Bill to suspend the trade and close the
harbour of the rebellious town. It was an unjust measure, as
foolish too as it was unjust, and was strongly opposed by Burke
and the other Whigs, who had not yet lost their heads over the
American question. So far as appearance went, it was at first
directed against Boston alone; but not content with this, the
ministry, with a folly which it is difficult to understand, proceeded
to pass what were known as the Regulation and Restriction Acts,
to regulate the government of the Province of Massachusetts Bay,
which destroyed the charter, and deprived the people of the
institutions and liberties to which they had become accustomed.
Thus they held up to every other colony the threat that the same
fate might befall them at any moment. By this simple expedient
they made the cause of Boston and of Massachusetts the cause of
every town and every colony on the Atlantic seaboard. The union
of the colonies was the one thing which was sure to prove fatal to
British supremacy. The policy of the Committee of Correspondence
had made this union possible. The action of the British ministry
made it inevitable.

In this way the struggle began, which was not only the most memorable event in the history of Boston, but one of the most memorable events of modern times, and which at the moment arrayed the forces of the British empire against this single colonial town. It was true that behind the town was the colony, and behind the colony of Massachusetts were the other twelve colonies, stretching from Maine to Georgia. It was true, also, that these thirteen colonies were soon to make common cause, and that the fate of one was to be the fate of all; but somewhere the first blow had to fall, and it was necessary that some community should stand up alone and meet the first shock. This was the lot of Boston; and her people entered upon the struggle with the same determination which they had exhibited in all the preliminary controversies. They must have perceived quite as plainly as we can see it now that much suffering was before them, that the odds against them were overwhelming, and that there were many things to be endured before the continent should be in arms; but they faced the situation unflinchingly, and refused to yield on any point. The policy of the ministry was emphasized by the removal of Hutchinson and the appointment of General Gage, who was also commander of the forces. This substitution of a soldier for a civilian indicated plainly enough what was intended; but nevertheless Hutchinson was so detested by his own people, who regarded him not only as an enemy but as a traitor, that they hailed his departure with rejoicing, and welcomed his successor, soldier though he was, with no little cordiality.

The Port Bill, which was really the first act of war on the part of England, fell upon Boston with cruel severity. As it was pre-eminently a trading town, with the cutting off of its commerce, all business practically ceased, the warehouses were empty, and the ships lay idle at the wharves. The only sails which now whitened the harbour were those of the English men-of-war, and even the ferries were not allowed to ply to the neighbouring towns. The other seaboard towns in Massachusetts, however, refused to take advantage of the misfortunes of the capital, and one and all united in sending relief to its inhabitants while they offered to its merchants the use of their wharves and storehouses. On the patriots' side actual government devolved largely on the Committee of Correspondence; and when the legislature met at Salem, for rebellious Boston could no longer be the seat of government, the one purpose in every one's mind was to take steps for calling a Continental Congress. Gage sent a messenger to dissolve the House, but the members held the door against him; and before his message was delivered they had issued a call to the other colonies. Then and not till then the legislature dissolved, to meet no more under the English Crown. Gage met this action, which really meant the severance of the British empire, with a proclamation against the non-importation agreement, which was more distinguished by bad temper than by anything else.

Soon after, in fact before the summer was half over, he carried out the Regulation and Restriction Acts, by which the provincial charter and all the institutions of Massachusetts were swept away. That which had been put in their place was shown by the appearance of large military forces, which were now necessary to sustain a government that had no popular support.

Four regiments and three companies of artillery were on Boston Common. Another regiment was at Fort Hill, and other companies at the Castle. Another regiment was at Salem, to protect the Government, whose source of power was in England; while still other troops were at Danvers, to watch over the governor. Thus, so far as proclamation could do it, the will of Parliament had been carried out; but the people of the colony had not yielded a jot, and the new acts had no effect beyond the lines of the English soldiers. The courts could not sit, for no jurors would serve, and the people paid no attention to the measures of Parliament, but busied themselves with methods for resisting them. Under the lead of Joseph Warren the county of Suffolk held a meeting, and adopted what were known as the Suffolk Resolves, in which all Parliamentary officers appointed under the acts were rejected, collectors of taxes were forbidden to pay money into the royal treasury, and towns were advised to choose only patriots for the militia; a Provincial Congress was also demanded, and obedience was promised to the Continental Congress. The people in these resolves, while they deprecated anything like riot or attacks upon property, threatened to seize every Crown officer if the governor should dare to arrest anybody; and they sent their resolutions in a memorial to the Continental Congress at Philadelphia, which recommended them to the people of the country at large as a practical method of meeting the crisis which had arisen.

Gage was not a particularly able man, nor was he a very good soldier; but in this state of affairs even Gage could see that war might come at any moment. He therefore began to seize the arms and munitions of war belonging to the Province, wherever he could lay his hand upon them, and to fortify Boston. He refused to let the legislature sit; and they accordingly resolved themselves into a Provincial Congress, and appointed a

Gage was not a particularly able man, nor was he a very good soldier; but even Gage could see that war might come. He therefore began to fortify Boston.

Committee of Safety and a Committee of Supplies, so that both sides were now arming with such ability as they possessed. New regiments came to Gage until he had some four to five thousand men under his command; and the Americans on their part began to enroll "minute-men" in every town, ready to resist the first attack. Gage attempted to stop this arming and collection of stores, but failed in the various expeditions which he sent out both to the north and south of Boston, until at last the time came when the inevitable blow was struck and the inevitable conflict begun.

In the early spring Gage determined to seize the cannon and other munitions of war belonging to the Province, which had been stored by the patriots at Concord; or, as some said at the time, he aimed to get possession of the persons of Samuel Adams and John Hancock. His movements to this end were conducted with as much secrecy as was possible to any military movement, and on the night of the 18th of April, eight hundred troops were embarked at the foot of Boston Common and rowed across to East Cambridge. The British supposed that this movement was unknown, although it is difficult to see how they could have imagined that such a thing could be possible. The proposed expedition was not only known, but the line of march as well, and exactly what was intended. The knowledge also was in the hands of men who knew what to do with it.

There were thirty mechanics of Boston who had enrolled themselves as a kind of volunteer committee to watch over the British. At their head was Paul Revere. When it was known that the British were intending to move, Revere crossed with his horse from Boston to Charlestown, and there saw the signal lantern, which had been already hoisted in the belfry of Christ Church, by a singular irony of fate, the Church of England and of Episcopacy. Revere, when he descried the light, at once mounted and rode away. His companion Rufus Dawes, who had started on the same errand, was stopped; but Revere eluded his pursuers and rode rapidly on through the night, arousing the people in the sleeping villages as he passed, until he had reached Concord. In the mean time, the troops sent out by Gage had started, and early in the morning of the 19th of April, a day forever memorable to the English-speaking world, they met a small and hastily gathered body of minute-men on the Green at Lexington. As the farmers and the soldiers faced each other, Major Pitcairn cried out, "Disperse, ye villains! ye rebels!" Then, as the rebels did not disperse, the troops fired. There was an irregular return of their shot, the handful of minute-men scattered, and war with England had begun.

After this affray, which could hardly be called even a skirmish, the British troops pressed on to Concord. The stores had been removed, and their errand was in vain. But again the minute-men turned out; and this time they stood their ground better and there was something more like a fight. British soldiers as well as American farmers were left dead upon the field, near the famous bridge, and then the British took up the line of their retreat to Boston. By this time the country was thoroughly aroused. From behind stone walls and trees along the whole line of march, the minute-men, fighting each man for himself, hung in ever-increasing numbers upon the flanks of the retreating army. The soldiers were unable to cope with them, or even to meet them; and dropped under their fire at every step. When the British reached Lexington they met Lord Percy, with reinforcements; and there sheltered by these fresh troops they threw themselves upon the ground, utterly worn out, having suffered severely along the whole line of their retreat.

Lord Percy and his detachment had left Boston early in the morning, having been ordered to start when it became known that the expedition of the night before had come to the knowledge of the patriots, who were prepared to meet it. He had marched out over Roxbury Neck, and thence across to Cambridge. As he passed through Boston and Roxbury with his band playing "Yankee Doodle," a boy in the streets called out, "You go out to 'Yankee Doodle' and you'll come back to 'Chevy Chase,'"—a more apt allusion to both the facts of the case and the family history of the Percys than the boy was probably aware. Delayed by the ill management which was characteristic of the British operations in America, Percy was too late to save the earlier expedition from a disastrous retreat; but he was in time to preserve them from absolute annihilation.

When the flying troops had been rescued and had rested, Percy took up again the line of march for Boston, making for the town this time by the way of Charlestown. The minute-men were on his flanks too, and troops from as distant points as Essex had reached his line of march. It was with difficulty that he succeeded in bringing his command into a place of safety; and he did not do even this without serious additional losses.

The fights of the 19th of April did more than bring on actual war between England and her colonies; they aroused the towns of Massachusetts and New England from one end to the other. The minute-men poured in from all directions and with so much rapidity that on the following day they were gathered about Boston in such numbers that Gage never sent out another expedition, and what is called the siege of Boston began. The English troops were shut up in what then constituted the city limits, which have now spread far beyond the territory occupied by Gage and his soldiers. If such a man as Robert Clive or Arthur Wellesley had been in Boston with four to five thousand men,

The great body of the inhabitants who sympathized with the patriot cause slipped out into the country, and all the scattered Tories, who were not very numerous, slipped in.

these fine English regiments with the command of the sea would never have remained there in feeble inactivity until they were at last driven to their boats in humiliation and defeat. They would have at least done some aggressive fighting. Every advantage of position, of equipment, of force, and of organization, belonged to the British. They had regular troops, well disciplined, well armed, furnished with every necessary of life, and supported by a fleet which had absolute command of the sea. Opposed to them were about twice the number of militia,—brave men undoubtedly, and ready to fight, but unorganized, undisciplined, without stores or munitions of war, and unaccustomed to battle. It was some time before the Americans were even put under a single command; and yet while Gage rested and did nothing, the minute-men made raids upon the outlying posts of Boston and upon the islands of the harbour, where they destroyed the houses and farms, carried off the British supplies, burned a schooner with four guns on board, and made the position of the invaders as uncomfortable as possible.

All that Gage and Howe did was to fortify the town carefully, a precaution which they took with the utmost thoroughness; while the great body of the inhabitants who sympathized with the patriot cause slipped out into the country, and all the scattered Tories, who were not very numerous, slipped in. This delay not only enabled the American generals to encourage their men by various successful raids, but also brought to them something like cohesion and the habit of acting together. There also came to Gage in the time of waiting powerful reinforcements under the command of Howe, Clinton, and Burgoyne, which raised his total force to some eleven thousand men; but still he neglected not only to assail the besiegers, but even to take possession of positions which commanded the town. The two principal points of this character were Dorchester Heights and Charlestown, lying respectively to the south and the north of the city, and both were neglected.

The Americans were more prompt. On the night of the 16th of June, General Ward, who was now in command of all the colonial forces, sent a detachment under Colonel Prescott, together with some Connecticut men under Captain Knowlton, to take possession of Charlestown. They stopped on the top of Bunker Hill, and then after some discussion decided to advance half a mile farther, to Breed's Farm, where the hill sloped toward the south, and whence they could command the town and shipping better. There they laid out a redoubt, at which they worked from midnight to eleven o'clock in the morning; while on the left they made a rude breastwork, which was known as the rail fence, at which the Connecticut men were stationed.

The British were alarmed at dawn by the sight of the redoubt, but the morning was far spent when they began to move, and it was noon when General Howe crossed with two thousand men and advanced against the breastworks on the hill. The Americans held their fire as the British came up the slope; and only when the troops were almost at the edge of the earthwork, did they open upon the British lines. The slaughter was terrible, and the British gave way in confusion; while their loss at the rail fence was even more severe. The Americans thought that all was over, and that they had nothing to do but pursue the flying foe; but their officers restrained them, knowing well that another assault would be made. Howe then had the village of Charlestown set on fire, re-formed his broken lines, and charged again. The result was the same, and if anything the loss was heavier. Again the Americans held their fire, delivering it at the last moment with terrible effect, and again the British fled in disorder, both from the fence and the redoubt. Once more Howe re-formed his line; and this time he advanced his field-pieces to the north, so as to rake the redoubt. He then charged again, telling his men to use only the bayonet. The Americans received them as before, and the British line staggered for a moment but the powder of the minute-men had given out, the redoubt was now open to the fire of the field-pieces on the north, and the colonists gave way as the British swarmed over the embankment. The last stand was made at the rail fence, where Stark of New Hampshire covered the retreat of the great body of the Americans. Prescott was furious that the reinforcements which had been promised had not been sent; but Ward can hardly be blamed for not sending troops when he knew, and did not dare to let any one else know, that there were only three rounds of powder to a man in the American camp.

Thus ended the battle of Bunker Hill. The British were in possession of the field; they had carried the position at the point of the bayonet, and the victory was technically theirs. Nevertheless, the real victory, and all the solid results of success, rested with the Americans. In the first place, although only a small number of troops had been engaged, the loss had been frightful on the side of the British. They had a thousand men killed and wounded, while the Americans had only lost between four and five hundred. Then it must also be remembered that the British troops fought with the greatest possible courage. A storming party in which a single company of one regiment lost every man in killed and wounded, is indubitable proof of the gallantry of the assault, and of the quality of the men who made it. The British superiority in discipline and numbers was balanced no doubt in part by the American advantage of position, and of fighting behind breastworks; but it is also true that the breastworks and the rail fence were defences of the flimsiest character, and served really for little more than to give to the militia the concentration and confidence which they might have lacked in the open field. Thus the odds were on the whole decidedly in favor of the British, and yet their loss more than doubled that of the colonists, while the difference in percentage of loss as compared with the total numbers engaged was still more to the advantage of the Americans. The greatest disaster to England, however, involved in the fight at Bunker Hill was the fact that it convinced the people of America that they could and would fight when they were put to it, and that they could defeat British troops if only they stood their ground. Washington, then on his way to take command of the American forces before Boston, knew in a moment what the single important point was in this battle. When the messenger bearing the news of Bunker Hill met him, the one question was, "Did the militia fight?" When he was told that they did fight, and how they fought, he said: "Then the liberties of the country are saved."

While the British were recovering from the shock of Bunker Hill, and the people who remained in Boston were looking for the first time on the grim sight of real war, Washington was posting, with all the speed that was possible, to take charge of the troops. He reached Cambridge on the 3d of July, and under the historic elm, drew his sword and took command of the soldiers gathered there, to regain the capital of New England. No longer were they minute-men, called hastily together to resist invasion, but the American Army; and the coming of Washington was the signal for the change. The battle, which Boston had begun, had become a national conflict, out of which a new nation was to arise.

Washington knew in a moment what the single important point was in this battle. When the messenger bearing the news of Bunker Hill met him, the one question was, "Did the militia fight?"

It is unnecessary here to trace in detail the history of the siege which followed; for the important part of that siege was enacted in the American lines outside of Boston, where Washington, grappling with immeasurable difficulties, tightened his grip upon the enemy in the town. There through the trying summer and winter he brought order out of chaos, and organization out of confusion. He turned rough militia companies into an effective fighting force, he concealed the lack of gunpowder, so that the British seemed never to have realized the almost helpless weakness of their opponents; he planned distant campaigns against other parts of the British domains, swept in munitions of war from every corner which he could reach, and finally sent Knox to bring guns from Ticonderoga across the snow, in the dead of winter, to Boston.

The English amused themselves after the fashion of a garrison, with balls and parties, and with plays, which were performed in Faneuil Hall.

In the mean time the British troops lived on in Boston, whence a very large proportion of the inhabitants had fled. There was illness and destitution in the town, and the British soldiers, by way of adding to the desolation of the time, pulled down houses for firewood and turned into a riding-school the church where generations had prayed, and where in recent years men had met in defence of their liberties.

Boston

The English amused themselves after the fashion of a garrison, with balls and parties, and with plays, which were performed in Faneuil Hall. They were more successful at these things than at fighting, or coping with the great soldier who held them in his grasp. They had eleven thousand men and a fleet of ships, and yet they allowed the genius of one man to shut them up in helpless inaction. They gave Washington time, and they could have given him no more precious gift; for, with time, he got his cannon and his gunpowder, and then he needed no waiting or suggestions to discover what he ought to do. In his impatience to assault the British, he already had proposed various plans of a more or less desperate character to his council; but now at last when he was armed, he moved rapidly forward upon the enemy.

On the evening of the 4th of March, 1776, after having kept up for a day or two a heavy cannonade to distract the attention of the besieged, he marched a body of men to Dorchester Heights, of which he took possession, and where he began at once to throw up intrenchments. There, under the eager leadership of Washington himself, the men worked all night long; and when morning came, the British, taken completely by surprise, beheld formidable works, growing every moment more impregnable, frowning over the town. Howe intended to attack them on Wednesday, but a storm came up; the men did not start, and afterward it was too late. Washington threatened to open fire, and by way of hint sent a few shots into the town. Thereupon, the English made up their minds that the end was upon them, but they continued to hesitate in action. Still Washington kept advancing his works; and on the 8th, Howe sent out a flag of truce, in which he assured Washington that he intended to withdraw, and that he would not injure the town, unless he was interfered with. Washington replied, saying that the assurance had no authority and bound no one. No other communication passed, however, and Washington did not attempt to push the bombardment seriously, as he felt confident that the British would retreat, and he did not wish to destroy the town. The result was that on the 17th of March, Howe, with his whole army, sailed away for Halifax, and the siege of Boston was at an end. Washington marched in at the head of the American troops, and then very soon marched away again, to carry the cause of the Revolution to victory in other parts of the continent.

So far as Boston was concerned, the fighting of the Revolution was over. The men of Boston and Massachusetts fought in every engagement, almost, of the six years of war which followed; but they had had their turn as a colony, and there was no more fighting on their own soil. They had been the first in the field, and had suffered proportionately. The flourishing colonial town, with more than twenty-five thousand inhabitants, which had celebrated with such rejoicing the repeal of the Stamp Act, was a dismal-looking place when Washington came in at the head of his victorious army. Houses had been burned and torn down in every direction. Pestilence and privation had done their work, and trade, industry, and commerce had been destroyed. The population was reduced to less than ten thousand people. The Patriots, who composed much the larger element of the population, had for the most part gone out at the beginning of the contest, and many never returned. When Howe sailed away, he took with him nearly a thousand persons who were attached to the Crown, while others of like predilections had slipped off in other directions.

This Tory emigration made a serious alteration in the character of the town. Most persons of wealth, the leaders in society and in politics in Boston, were Royalists, and remained loyal to England. When they went, they left a great gap. The only one of their number who had been conspicuous on the Patriot side was John Hancock. Samuel Adams was of old Puritan stock, but was not identified with the rich and office-holding classes of Boston. The other men who led in the Revolution were from the counties; and it was from the counties that the people came who filled the places of the Tories who had gone. The loyalists who remained in Boston were few in number, and kept themselves very quiet; while the society which arose after the Revolution was composed of the leaders from the smaller towns, and from the country. The merchants of Salem and Newburyport, the squires and magistrates and judges of the interior counties were the men who now came to the capital and took the places of the leaders who had either departed or been discredited. In the country everybody high and low, with but few exceptions, espoused the Patriot cause, for in Massachusetts the Tory element was almost wholly confined to a single large town; and it was therefore upon that town that the loss of population entailed by civil war fell.

In this way it came about that the society which grew up in Boston after the Revolution was chiefly made up of persons who were not identified with the Boston of the colonial and provincial days. The body of the population which came in, also came from the country. Many of them were families who simply returned to their old dwelling-places; others were people who had before lived in some outlying town, and who now came to Boston to better their condition, or for some similar reason. But the siege marked a great change in the life of Boston. It went into the struggle with England a rich, thriving provincial town, with a fashionable society attached to the Crown, and a rich Puritan element, not, perhaps, given to all the ways of Crown officials, but equally loyal to the English Government. It came out with its population reduced more than one half, and with its upper class swept away, while those who remained were weakened by disease, and impoverished by the long occupation of foreign troops and the cessation of all business. Boston had done its work in the American Revolution, and had paid a heavy price in the short time that it had been engaged. It really seemed as if the growth and progress of nearly a hundred years had been overthrown in the few months of the struggle with England. But the people set themselves to putting their homes in order, and to repairing their broken fortunes with characteristic energy; so that the town began to rally slowly but surely from its misfortunes. The tide of war did not again break upon Boston, so that it had time to collect itself, and to gather strength for future successes, even while the Revolution was still in progress, and before peace came to bring once more security to business and prosperity to the people.

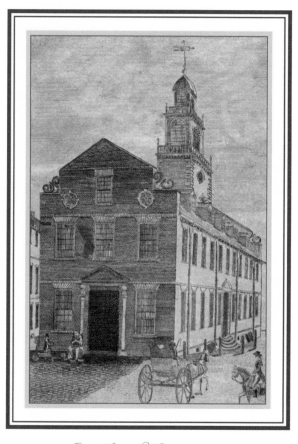

Old State House 1791

10. Federalist Boston.

TEN YEARS elapsed before the population reached the point at which it stood prior to the Revolution; and in that decade both town and State had much to endure in settling the legacies always bequeathed to a community by civil strife. The adjustment of social, financial, and political balances, after such a wrenching of the body politic, was a slow and in some respects a harsh and trying process, and many years passed before a condition of stable equilibrium was again attained.

In the provincial times, although the political system and theory of Massachusetts were democratic, there was a vigorous and powerful aristocracy holding all the appointed and many of the elective offices, and recognized as leaders in public affairs. As a rule, this provincial aristocracy, which had its headquarters in Boston, was strongly in sympathy with the Crown, and abandoned the country on the success of the Patriots, either in the great flight which took place when Howe evacuated Boston, or singly, when opportunity offered. Their estates were confiscated, and they themselves took refuge for the most part in the northern provinces, and sometimes in England; but wherever they were, their loyalty was remembered, and they were aided by the English government. Here and there exceptions to this rule could, of course, be found,—as notably in the case of John Hancock and the Quincys; although even in the latter family of Patriots one distinguished member was a Tory, and went into exile in consequence. There were a few others of this class who, while their sympathies were with England, managed to preserve a judicious neutrality, and remained in their native town, suspected by many, and stripped of all political power, but retaining their social position, and after many years regaining some portion of their influence. These remnants of the provincial aristocracy however were at best insignificant, and new men had ample openings in the great gaps which war had made. The new men, of course, came; and equally, of course, they were the leaders of the successful Revolution. They were not, however, as commonly happens in such cases, drawn from the class immediately below that which had been overthrown. The country aristocracy, the squires and gentry of the small towns and villages, unlike their brethren of the capital, had been as a rule on the side of resistance to England, and had furnished most of the Revolutionary leaders. When their battle was won, many of them came up from their

counties and settled in Boston, occupying the places of their
banished opponents, and not infrequently by cheap purchases
becoming possessors of the confiscated homes of the exiles. To this
class, which, to borrow a very famous name, may be not inaptly
styled the Country party, belonged, for example, the Adamses and
Fisher Ames from Norfolk, the Prescotts from Middlesex, and the
Sullivans from New Hampshire; while from Essex, most prolific of
all, came the Parsonses, Pickerings, Lees, Jacksons, Cabots,
Lowells, Grays, and Elbridge Gerry. These men and their families
rapidly filled the places left vacant in society by the old supporters
of the Crown, and, of course, already possessed the political power
which they had gained by the victories of the Revolution. This new
aristocracy maintained for many years the ascendency in public
affairs which had been held by their predecessors, but their
tenure, weakened by the ideas developed in the Revolution, was
more precarious; and although they dictated the policy of the
State for nearly half a century, their power as a class broke down
and disappeared before the rapid rise and spread of democracy
during the lifetime of the next generation.

The Patriot party, the Whigs of the Revolution, triumphed so
completely by the result of the war that they found themselves not
only masters of the field in 1782, but absolutely unopposed. In
their own numbers party divisions were in due time formed, and

we can detect the germ of those divisions, even before the peace, in the convention which met at Boston in 1780 to frame a constitution for Massachusetts. The old chiefs as a rule leaned, as might be expected, to popular and democratic views; but what was more important, they belonged, like Sam Adams, to the class of minds which can destroy, but which cannot construct. The

The old chiefs belonged, like Sam Adams, to the class of minds which can destroy, but which cannot construct.

younger leaders, on the other hand, belonged to the coming period of reconstruction, when a new fabric of politics and society was to be built up, and were more conservative and less democratic than those whom they had followed in the conflict with England. The first serious division of opinion in the Patriot party grew out of the difficulties engendered by the war. The heaviest burdens were financial. Debts, public and private, weighed severely upon the State, and upon nearly every member of the community. General insolvency, in fact, prevailed. The war had drained the country of specie; the Continental paper was worthless, and that of the State not much better. The scarcity of a decent circulating medium was in fact so great that payments in kind were legalized. To thinking men it was already obvious that a strong central government, stability, order in the public finances, and a vigorous administration, both State and National, were essential to drag the country out of the chaos of floating debts, repudiation, and irredeemable currency, and to knit once more the political bonds, almost dissolved by war. To effect such results was no easy matter. Society and public opinion had been grievously shaken, and old habits had been loosened and weakened.

As always happens in times of distress and depression, there were many among the more ignorant of the community who mistook effect for cause. They were poor and in debt; and in the means adopted by their creditors to collect debts through the usual legal machinery, they believed they saw the source of their sufferings. The popular feeling of discontent in the western part of Massachusetts, therefore, began as early as 1782 to express itself in resistance to law and to the courts. Matters went on from bad to worse; violence and force became more and more common; the power of the State was crippled; and at last it all culminated in the insurrection known in our history as Shays's Rebellion, which was directed against the courts and the enforcement of the laws, and which not only threatened the existence of the commonwealth, but shook to its foundations the unstable fabric of the Confederacy. While the storm was gathering, John Hancock, the popular hero and governor, not fancying the prospect opening before the State, and the consequent difficulties and dangers likely to beset the chief magistrate, took himself out of the way, and the younger and more conservative element in politics elected James Bowdoin in his stead. It was a fortunate choice in every way. Bowdoin was a wise, firm, courageous man, perfectly ready to sacrifice popularity, if need be, to the public good. He was warmly supported in Boston, as the principles and objects of Shays and his followers were peculiarly obnoxious to a business community. The alarm in the town was very great, for it looked as if their contest for freedom was about to result in anarchy. The young men came forward, armed themselves, and volunteered for service; but the governor's firmness was all that was needed, and General Lincoln, at the head of the militia, easily crushed the feeble mob gathered by Shays, whose followers were entirely dispersed. Nevertheless, the rioters represented, although in a very extreme fashion, the general sentiment of the State, demoralized and shaken by civil war; and this fact was shown by the almost criminal delay of the lower branch of the legislature in sustaining the governor in his efforts to maintain order, and by their reluctance to declare the insurgents in rebellion,—a step forced upon them by the vigour of the governor and senate. This unhappy condition of public opinion was still more strongly manifested at the next election. The issue was made up between pardon and sympathy for the rebels on the one side, and just and salutary punishment on the other. The conservative party, in favour of the latter course, put forward Bowdoin; while Hancock, who had been under shelter, now came forward once more to catch the popular support as the advocate of mercy, which another and braver man had alone earned the right to dispense. Hancock had chosen his time well. Popular feeling in the country districts was with the insurgents, and Bowdoin was defeated; although Boston, now thoroughly in the hands of the younger and more conservative party, strongly sustained him. Thus the new party of order and reconstruction started in Boston, which continued to be its headquarters, and gradually extending its influence, first through the eastern towns, and then to the west, came finally to control the State.

The Shays Rebellion was without doubt an efficient cause in promoting the convention at Philadelphia which framed the constitution of the United States.

The Shays Rebellion did more, however, than decide the elections in Massachusetts. It was without doubt an efficient cause in promoting the convention at Philadelphia which framed the constitution of the United States, and in frightening into concurrent action the decrepit and obstructive Congress of the Confederation. The ratification of the constitution submitted by the delegates who met in Philadelphia to establish a central government and a better union of the States was an event of national as well as local importance, for the adhesion of the great State of Massachusetts was essential to success. Boston was the scene of the protracted struggle in the State convention, which was held to consider this momentous question, first in Brattle Street Church, still bearing the marks of Washington's cannon, later in the State House, and later still in the meeting-house in Long Lane. The town itself was, of course, deeply interested in the result, and was strongly in favour of the constitution; but the details of the long conflict which ended in its ratification by Massachusetts, do not immediately concern this history. The conservative elements, which had begun to take a party shape in the Shays Rebellion, then and there developed into a strong and homogeneous body in support of the constitution. They had an arduous battle to fight, and they fought it well. Against them were arrayed all the sympathizers with the late insurrection, besides many who had actually taken part in it, and who, having tasted the sweets of incipient anarchy, were averse to anything like strong government. There can be no doubt that at the outset public feeling and a majority of the convention were against the constitution, while at the same time the great leaders of the revolutionary period, Hancock and Adams, were lukewarm. By ability in debate, by perseverance, by managing and flattering Hancock, these difficulties were gradually overcome; while to gain the earnest and active support of Adams, the popular sentiment of Boston was invoked. The mechanics of the town, under the lead of Paul Revere, held a great meeting at the Green Dragon Tavern, on Union Street, and passed resolutions in favour of the constitution. This was the voice of an oracle to which Adams had often appealed in trying times; and its utterance now weighed with him, and changed cool and critical approval to active support. Perhaps it decided the fate of the constitution; for the great influence of Adams may well have counted for much in a close majority of only nineteen votes.

The adoption of the constitution by Massachusetts was a source of profound satisfaction to Boston, and was celebrated with great rejoicing. With intense interest Boston watched the ratification of the constitution by one State after another; and we can see, in the newspapers, the rapid development of the new party of reconstruction, the friends of the constitution, now known as Federalists, and the corresponding increase of bitterness toward all who attempted to thwart a measure believed, in Boston at least, to involve the future existence of the nation. The party which thus took shape in the debates of the constitutional convention, and which was solidified and strengthened by victory, bent all its energies to selecting senators and representatives who were well known to be strong friends of the new scheme. Flushed with their first triumph, the Federalists were generally successful, and both senators were tried friends of the constitution. But their most signal victory was in the Boston District, where they elected Fisher Ames the young and eloquent champion of the constitution over Samuel Adams, the veteran of the Revolution, and the idol of the town, but now suspected of coolness toward the great instrument which was destined to be the corner-stone of a nation. The defeat of Adams by Ames marked Boston as the great centre of New England Federalism.

The pleasure excited in Boston by the successful establishment of the new government found an opportunity for expression when Washington, venerated and beloved, the mainstay of the Union, as he had been of the Revolution, made his visit to Massachusetts in the autumn of 1789. The President, accompanied by the Vice-President, John Adams, was received by the authorities on the outskirts of the town, and having been presented with an address, rode through the streets on a fine white horse, escorted by a long procession, civil and military, and greeted on all sides by the applause of a dense crowd. On arriving at the State House he was conducted to a platform thrown out on the west side of the building, and arranged, as we are informed, "to exhibit in a strong light the MAN OF THE PEOPLE." As Washington stood forth in all his simple majesty, cheers rang out, and an ode was sung in his honour by singers placed in a triumphal arch close by. After this the procession broke up, and then for several days there was a round of dinners and state visits.

Washington lived during his stay in Boston at the corner of Tremont and Court Streets, where a small tablet still commemorates his sojourn. The most amusing incident of this visit, and the one most characteristic both of the men and the times, was the little conflict between him and John Hancock on a point of etiquette, which had a good deal more real importance than such points generally possess. Hancock, as the chief officer of what he esteemed a sovereign State, undertook to regard Washington as a sort of foreign potentate, who was bound to pay the first visit to the ruler of the Commonwealth in which he found himself, while Washington took the view that he was the superior officer of the Governor of Massachusetts, and that, as the head of the Union, Hancock was bound to visit him first. Washington's sense of dignity, and of what was due to his position, had often been exemplified, and the governor's vanity and State sovereignty were no match for it. Hancock prudently made the gout an excuse for giving way; and having as fine a sense as the first Pitt of the theatrical properties of his malady, he appeared at Washington's door, swathed in flannel, and was borne on men's shoulders to the President's apartments. After this all went well; and Washington's visit not only drew out the really vigorous personal loyalty of the people, but still further kindled the enthusiasm of Boston and of New England for the Union, and consequently strengthened the hands of the Federalists.

Boston became the centre of many great schemes for public improvements, most of which came to nothing, although they served, nevertheless, to encourage the business of the town.

The assumption of the State debts by the new Federal government did much to relieve the financial burdens of Massachusetts; and this, combined with the sense of stability in public affairs, roused the spirit of enterprise everywhere, so that Boston became the centre of many great schemes for public improvements, most of which came to nothing, although they served, nevertheless, to encourage the business of the town. The population had again reached the number which it had before the Revolution, and the new era to which the war had been a prelude was fairly begun. As if to mark the change which had set in, one of the most conspicuous characters of the old period passed away at this time, by the death of John Hancock. There have been but few men in history who have achieved so much fame, and whose names are so familiar, who at the same time really did so little, and left so slight a trace of personal influence upon the times in which they lived, as John Hancock. He was valuable chiefly from his picturesqueness. Everything about him was picturesque, from his bold, handsome signature, which gave him an assured immortality on the Declaration of Independence, to his fine house, which appears in the pictures of the day as the "Seat of His Excellency, John Hancock." His position, wealth, and name made him valuable to the real movers of the Revolution, when men of his stamp were almost without exception on the side of the Crown; and it was this which made such a man as Samuel Adams cling to and advance him, and which gave him a factitious importance. Hancock was far from greatness; indeed it is to be feared that he was not much removed from being "the empty barrel," which is the epithet, tradition says, that the outspoken John Adams applied to him. Yet he had a real value after all. He was the Alcibiades, in a certain way, of the rebellious little Puritan town; and his display and gorgeousness no doubt gratified the

sober, hard-headed community which put him at its head and
kept him there. He stands out with a fine show of lace and velvet
and dramatic gout,—a real aristocrat, shining and resplendent
against the cold gray background of everyday life in the Boston
of the days after the Revolution, when the gay official society of
the Province had been swept away. At the side of his house he
built a dining hall, where he could assemble fifty or sixty guests;
and when his company was gathered he would be borne or
wheeled in, and with easy grace would delight every one by his
talk and finished manners. In society his pettiness, peevishness,
and narrowness would vanish, and his true value as a brilliant and
picturesque figure would come out.

Hancock's death was but one of the incidents which, as the
old century hastened to its close, marked the change which had
fairly come. The old simplicity, as well as the old stateliness and
pomp, were alike slipping away. Those were the days when the
gentry lived in large houses, enclosed by handsome gardens, and
amused themselves with card-parties, dancing-parties, and
weddings, and when there were no theatres, and nothing in the
way of relaxation except these little social festivities. But the
enemy was at the gates,—a great, hurrying, successful, driving
democracy. Brick blocks threatened the gardens; the theatre
came, despite the august mandate of Governor Hancock; the

elaborate and stately dress of the eighteenth century began to be pushed aside, first for grotesque and then for plainer fashions; the little interests of provincial days began to wane; Unitarianism sapped the foundations of the stout old church of Winthrop and Cotton; and the eager zest for intellectual excitement poured itself into business and politics (the only channels then open), giving to the latter an intensity hardly to be appreciated in days when mental resources are as numerous as they then were few. Boston was feeling the effects of the change which had been wrought by the War for Independence, the first act of the mighty revolutionary drama just then reopening in Paris.

To this change and progress in society and in habits of life the French Revolution gave of course a powerful impetus. The tidings from Paris were received in this country at first with a universal burst of exultation, which found as strong expression in Boston as anywhere. The success of Dumouriez was the occasion of a great demonstration. A liberty pole was raised, an ox roasted, and bread and wine distributed in State Street; while Samuel Adams, who had succeeded his old companion as governor, presided, with the French consul, at a great civic banquet in Faneuil Hall. The follies of the Parisian mob were rapidly adopted; "Liberty and Equality" was stamped on children's cakes, and the sober merchants and mechanics of Boston began to address each other as "citizen"

Brown, and "citizen" Smith. The ridiculous side of all this business would soon have made itself felt among a people whose sense of humour was one of their strongest characteristics; but when the farce became tragedy, and freedom was baptized in torrents of blood, and the gentle, timid, stupid king, known to Americans only as a kind friend, was brought to the block, the enthusiasm rapidly subsided. Every one knows how the affairs of France were dragged into our national politics for party purposes, with Democratic societies and Jacobin clubs in their train, and the bitterness which came from them; but all this gained little foothold in Boston, where the insults of Genet, the first minister of revolutionary France, roused general indignation, and the attitude of Washington toward the insolent Frenchman found hearty support.

When Samuel Adams retired from public life, the growth of the Federalist party was shown by the choice of Increase Sumner as his successor. Governor Sumner was an ardent supporter of John Adams,—then just beginning his eventful administration; and the troubles with France which ensued, awakened deep indignation in Boston. Sumner's course drew out the most violent attacks, but he was re-elected nevertheless, by an overwhelming majority. The fortunes of the Federalists were at their highest point; and Moses Gill,—the lieutenant-governor—whom the death of Sumner left at the head of the government—was succeeded by Caleb Strong, an ex-senator, and one of the staunchest of Federalists. Yet even in the midst of their success, the hour of their downfall was at hand. The administration of John Adams was torn with fierce internal dissensions, and the President and the leaders in New England were hopelessly estranged. But although many of the chiefs in Boston drew off from the President, the clans stood by him, and gave him the vote of Massachusetts. It proved a useless loyalty. The Federalists fell from power, and the new century opened with the accession of Jefferson, an event which both leaders and followers in Boston had brought themselves to believe would be little else than the coming of a Marat or a Robespierre. It is hardly necessary to say that nothing of this sort happened; but that, on the contrary, a period of prosperity, for which the short-lived peace of Amiens opened the way, began, as unequalled as it was unexpected. This prosperity took the form of maritime commerce, and poured its riches into the lap of Boston,

The new century opened with the accession of Jefferson, an event which leaders in Boston had brought themselves to believe would be little else than the coming of a Marat or a Robespierre.

conspicuously among all the seaports. At the same time, of course, all the country throve, although the great advance was most apparent among the merchants of Boston and New York, and the seafaring population of New England. When men are making money and prospering, it is not easy to awaken among them great political enthusiasm, nor is it easy to convince them that the administration under which they have succeeded is a bad one. But this was not the case with the Federalist leaders. Nothing could check their deadly hatred of Jefferson, which increased as they saw their own power decline and that of the Government wax strong. As the conviction forced itself upon their minds that the sceptre of government had passed finally to the South, before whom a divided North was helpless, they struggled vainly against fate; and the bitterness of party, so marked in the first decade of the century, found its origin in the years of Jefferson's first term, when peace and prosperity reigned throughout the country. Like the Whig party in England, after the fall of the Coalition, when they were called to face Pitt and his vast majorities, the thin ranks of the Federalists were still further weakened by the internal dissensions growing out of the sorry strifes of the Adams administration. These quarrels had been allayed by defeat; but they were only partially healed, and they were soon to bear bitter fruit. Of all this, Boston was of course the centre; and when the annexation of Louisiana roused the Federalists to desperation, it was in Boston that a meeting was to be held, at which Hamilton should be present, and where the schemes of secession which the New England leaders had been seriously discussing under their breath should find expression, and obtain a decision on their merits. The good sense of some of the leaders contributed with other causes to prevent the occurrence of this meeting; but had there been no other obstacle, the death of Hamilton would have sufficed to cause postponement, if nothing else. The loss of that great man was peculiarly felt in Boston, where almost every man of note was one of his devoted followers, and where Federalism had struck its roots deeper and clung with a greater tenacity than anywhere else. In Boston, Hamilton's death was deeply mourned. There the money, a large sum for those days, was subscribed to buy his lands and relieve the necessities of his family; and there the first statue of later times was raised to the great secretary, commemorating alike his genius and the enduring and faithful Federalism of the old town in the years when the power of the Democratic party seemed universal.

In this dark hour the Federalists were, indeed, nearly extinct; and when Massachusetts, in 1804, gave her electoral vote to

Jefferson, it seemed as if the end could not be far distant. In fact, the Federalist party would soon have perished utterly had it not been for the amazing blunders of Jefferson's second term, which gave them a new lease of life and a vigorous and partially successful existence.

But the fervour of partisan feeling was soon to glow with a still fiercer heat, owing to the course of the world's history, in which the United States, the only neutral nation, and still shackled by colonial feelings, was the football of the two great contending forces, Napoleon Bonaparte and the English Government. Into the stream of these mighty events, which were world-wide in their scope, the fortunes of Boston were strongly drawn.

The renewal of hostilities by Napoleon had thrown the trade of all nations, and particularly that of England, the dominant power of the commercial world, into confusion. From this disorder the United States, as the only neutral with a strong merchant-marine, reaped a rich harvest, the fruits of which fell of course largely to New England, and therefore to Boston. It was the golden era of the American merchant-service, in which much of the best ability and the most daring enterprise were concentrated. Always alert and now flushed with success, the New England sea-captains and the merchants of Boston took quick advantage of the troubles of Europe to engross rapidly the carrying-trade of the world, and to heap up handsome fortunes from its enormous profits. Our success and prosperity after the outbreak of war in Europe were in truth too obvious, and soon aroused the unsleeping jealousy of England. Seizures began to be made by British cruisers; then came unwarrantable condemnations in the British admiralty courts; and then oppressive Orders in Council. The first sensation was one of angry pride and keen disappointment at interference with our apparently boundless sources of profit. Sharp remonstrances and resolutions went out from Boston to spur the lagging Executive. The Federalist leaders, who regarded England as the bulwark of civilization against the all-destroying French Revolution personified in Napoleon, were overborne; and, while reprobating these violent measures in secret, seemed about to lose their last hold upon the people, and were forced to see their governor, Caleb Strong, replaced by James Sullivan, a leading Democrat. They were properly helpless before the righteous indignation which blazed up more fiercely than ever when the English, not content with despoiling our merchant-vessels, fired upon the national flag flying from a national ship. If Mr. Jefferson had at that supreme moment declared war, and appealed to the country, he would have had the cordial support of the mass of the people not only in New England but in Boston itself, the very citadel of Federalism. But it was not to be. The President faltered as the Federalists rallied and renewed their attack, fell back on his preposterous theories of commercial warfare, well suited to his timidity and love of shuffling, and forced the celebrated embargo through both Houses of Congress. The support of New England in the trying times which were at hand was lost to the Administration, and the political game in that important section of the country was once more in the hands of those Federalist chiefs whose headquarters were at Boston. The Federalism of Boston had in fact remained steady in every trial, although there was a moment when Jefferson might have sapped its strength. It had been heard in Washington for years through the eloquent lips of Josiah Quincy, whose voice now rose clearer and stronger than ever, trumpet-tongued against the embargo policy. The defection of John Quincy Adams on this same measure gave the town another strong and outspoken representative in the Senate in the person of James Lloyd, a leading merchant; and thus equipped in Washington, Boston faced the impending troubles.

So bitter however was the feeling against England, so strong the sense of wounded national pride, that even the embargo was received in Boston at first with silent submission; but its operation told so severely upon both town and State that hostility to the Administration rapidly deepened and strengthened. We can now hardly realize the effect of this measure upon Boston; but one fact lets in a flood of light. The tonnage of the United States in 1807 was, in round numbers, eight hundred and fifty thousand tons, and of this three hundred and ten thousand tons belonged to Massachusetts alone. The total cessation of commerce fell therefore upon Boston with blighting effect. Her merchant-ships rotted at the wharves, or were hauled up and dismantled.

The busy ship-yards were still and silent, and all who gained their living by them were thrown out of work. The fisheries were abandoned, and agriculture was distressed. If in Philadelphia seamen marched in large bodies to the City Hall for relief, we can imagine what the condition of the seafaring population must have been in Boston. Ruin threatened the merchants, and poverty stared the labouring classes in the face. Gradually all this began to tell upon the temper of the people; riots and insurrections were feared by men of all parties; and the Federalists now found willing listeners when they pointed out to a people naturally brave and ready to fight, that the injuries inflicted by England were trifling in comparison with the total destruction of trade caused by their own Government; that the embargo had not as usual a limitation, but might become permanent; and that however it might be disguised, the only people really benefited by the embargo were the French. Slowly political power returned to the party constantly in opposition to Jefferson and all his works. Resistance began to crop out on all sides. Pickering attacked Governor Sullivan in a violent pamphlet; Samuel Dexter argued in court against the constitutionality of the embargo, and juries refused to convict for infractions of its provisions. The Federalists carried the legislature, and passed resolutions denouncing the embargo, and questioning its constitutionality; while the town of Boston instructed its representatives, in town meeting, to resist the hated law, in terms which recalled the days of Samuel Adams and the Port Bill, and which induced John Randolph to remind Jefferson of the fate of Lord North in a former difficulty with the Puritan town. Then it was that John Quincy Adams thought treason and secession were afoot in Boston, and warned the Administration of its peril. He was mistaken as to the extent of the danger, for there was no treason, and nothing worse than ominous whisperings of secession. The ripeness of the times and of the public, in Boston, for desperate measures was sufficient to excite such suspicions; but the Federalists did not aim at violence. In the state of society then existing, in the opportunity offered, and in the condition of the times, it is a matter of wonder that passions were so controlled; for it is not easy to appreciate now the mental concentration in that day and generation. There was practically no art, no literature, no science of native origin; the only great branch of business was laid low by the embargo, and there were none of the thousand and one interests which now divide and absorb our energy and activity. Absolutely, the only source of intellectual excitement was politics; and to this were confined the mental forces of a small, vigorous, cultivated, and aristocratic society, which flung itself into public affairs with its whole heart and soul. They were a convivial set, these Federalist leaders in Boston, and were wont to dine together at three o'clock; and at five, when the ladies left the room, Madeira and politics flowed without stint until midnight and after. It is small wonder that their politics were heated; that ex-senators and governors bandied harsh words in the offices of State Street, or demanded explanations in the newspapers; and that the traditional

There was practically no art, no literature, no science of native origin; the only source of intellectual excitement was politics.

feuds and bitterness of 1808, although softened and apparently forgotten, have survived in Boston among those who inherit them even to the present day.

With matters in this state, the passage of the enforcing act aroused so much anger, the attitude of New England became so menacing, that the Northern Democrats quailed; and led by such "pseudo Republicans" as Joseph Story who were not ready to sacrifice their homes to Mr. Jefferson's theories, Congress repealed the embargo. There was a great sigh of relief; and when the Erskine arrangement was made, the sails of the merchant-ships again whitened the harbour of Boston. The more reasonable policy of Mr. Madison was only temporary, however, in its effects, and was soon replaced by vacillation, and by labyrinthine complications into which it is unnecessary to enter. Still, the relaxation, slight as it was, sufficed to loosen the hold of the Federalists, and Governor Gore was replaced by Elbridge Gerry, whose administration was in itself enough to strengthen and to give victory once more to its opponents. He denounced in a message the publications of the Federal press, which were, indeed, vituperative and coarse to a high degree, especially in Boston; and he endeavoured to bring in the power of the government to punish the aggressors. He also supported a plan of arranging election districts for partisan purposes, which was so bad, and at that time so unheard of, that it gave a new word to the language. All this enabled the Federalists to defeat him by a close vote, in which they were aided by the gathering clouds of conflict, which finally broke, June 18, 1812, in Mr. Madison's declaration of war against England.

Boston

The effect of the war on Boston was severe in the extreme. Not only was commerce the great source of industry and wealth wholly cut off, but the dependence upon England now so difficult to realize not only for every manufactured article of luxury but for many of the necessaries of life, had, by the cessation of intercourse, brought a sense of privation and loss into every household. The war, and the policy of commercial restriction preceding it, had also upon Boston one deep and lasting effect, which was hardly perceived at the moment, but which changed her business character, and powerfully influenced her politics from that day to this. In the first years of the nineteenth century, Boston was a great commercial centre, and nothing else. Mr. Jefferson with his embargo and its kindred measures, followed as they were by the War of 1812, shook the whole financial and economical system of the town. Commerce was crippled, at times almost extinguished, and comparatively large masses of capital were set loose and left idle, while at the same time an immense fund of enterprise and activity was unemployed. The result was to force all this capital and enterprise into other channels, where before they had begun to flow very slowly. Manufactures received a great impetus; and the capital, which had been turned aside by the policy of the Administration, did not, when peace came, revert to its old pursuits. From being a strong free-trade town, Boston became as vigorously protectionist before the first quarter of a century closed. Mr. Jefferson seems to have designed to reduce the commercial interest and weaken New England by his policy; he certainly regarded with complacency the fact that it would have that tendency. The result, however, was that manufactures were stimulated. The progress of Boston was changed, not arrested; and New England industries were for years protected, as Jefferson's political followers believed, at the expense of his beloved South.

Almost coincident with the disappearance of the Federalist party was the change from the town form to that of a city.

The conclusion of the war, and the revival of business in all directions, closed the differences which had divided the country since the foundation of the government, and turned men's minds from the political issues of the past. It was the dawn of the so-called era of good-feeling, the transition period, in which old parties disappeared and new ones were developed. The Federalists of Massachusetts retained their power for many years, dexterously avoiding the rocks of religious controversy on which their party brethren of Connecticut were wrecked. They held the government by reason of past services solely, for the great political questions which had brought them forth and given them strength no longer existed. Gradually, however, they faded away; the old leaders in Boston and elsewhere retired from public life, or were removed by death; and the century had hardly completed its second decade when the great party of Washington, really lifeless for some years, vanished even in name from our history, finally and irrevocably.

Almost coincident with the disappearance of the Federalist party was the change of municipal government in Boston from the town form to that of a city. The change had been agitated at various times from a very early period down to 1821, and in the next year the old town government came to an end. It had been the government of Winthrop and Cotton, of Adams and Franklin; it had defied George III. and Lord North, and its name had rung through two continents in the days when it faced the English Parliament alone and unterrified; it was the most famous municipal organization in America, and it passed away into history honoured and regretted.

View of Boston in 1848

11. The City of Boston.

WHEN BOSTON passed from a system of town government to that of a city, it passed from one form of local government to another equally well known to English-speaking people, although not so ancient. The direct government by the people themselves, meeting together to decide upon their own affairs, was replaced by a representative system on the model of English cities, with which the people of Boston in knowledge if not in practice had always been familiar. Instead of a meeting of the people, the City had a Board of Aldermen and a Common Council to legislate for them; and instead of the Selectmen, there was a Mayor to execute the orders of the representative body and to administer the government. The change although long resisted, and at the last carried only by a slender majority, had become absolutely necessary owing to the growth of the population. Matters of general interest were sure to receive a fairer and better consideration at the hands of a representative body than they could possibly obtain from a town-meeting where only a small fragment of the forty thousand inhabitants could be present, and where that small fragment had neither representative authority nor responsibility. Thus it came about that much as the change was regretted and opposed, it was accepted as inevitable, and the people soon adapted themselves to it.

The first mayor under the new charter was John Phillips, chosen to that office because there had been dissensions among the Federalists (then in their last days, but still powerful in Boston) as to the candidate whom they should put up. The result of the wrangle was a compromise by general assent upon Mr. Phillips; and the election of the mayor was neither advocated nor opposed very strongly by anybody. Mr. Phillips held office only for a year, and then was succeeded by Josiah Quincy, who left a deeper imprint upon the Government of Boston than any man who has been connected with it since the city charter went into effect. Mr. Quincy had distinguished himself in earlier days in Washington as a member of

Josiah Quincy left a deeper imprint upon the Government of Boston than any man who has been connected with it since the city charter went into effect.

Congress, where he had been the ablest and most eloquent leader of the irreconcilable Federalists. He was a man of marked qualities and well-defined ideas, very determined and, like most strong men, inclined to be arbitrary. He had, what few mayors have, a policy of a broad and far-reaching kind; and he had in addition, what is possessed by still fewer, the energy, the determination, and the power to carry that policy into effect. The first year of the city system under Mr. Phillips's somewhat timid leadership did not meet the expectations of the people as to the benefits of their new form of government, but they had no such complaint to make in the case of Mr. Quincy. During his five years of rule, the sanitary condition of the city was made better, the work of cleaning the streets was systematized, the police force was improved, a new market was built which had the effect of opening up the lower part of Boston, and the fire department was reorganized and made as efficient as the methods of that day permitted. Mr. Quincy also carried through measures for the better care of the poor, and advanced very much the standard of education in the schools. He performed during his years of office a really great work; but like most men who carry through important reforms and novel measures, he gradually raised up so many enemies that he was defeated for his sixth term. Nevertheless, it is to him that Boston really owes her organization as a city; for by him the enactments of the charter were converted into living and moving realities. It was he who marked out the lines on which the city in the main has proceeded since; and to him Boston owes a debt which she ought never to forget.

Quincy's successor was Harrison Gray Otis, who, like Quincy, had been for many years distinguished in public life and a leader of the Federalist party. His descent from one of the families most distinguished in the previous century for leading the resistance to England, his own eminence in public life, his wealth, his brilliancy as an orator, combined with a remarkable grace of manner, made him for many years the most conspicuous figure in Boston society. It so happened that he was ill on the day of his inauguration. He therefore sent for the aldermen and the common council to come to his house, where he read to them his inaugural address, and had the City Government for the ensuing year duly although privately organized,—an evidence of social power which would be no longer possible.

The practice of taking for mayor the citizen most distinguished socially and politically, as illustrated in the election of Quincy and Otis, was of short duration. City politics soon took on another and more democratic form. National parties were extended to municipal affairs, an illogical but perhaps inevitable arrangement, which has been productive of much evil, and which has led to independent combinations, known generally as "citizens' tickets," for the purpose of defeating the candidates of the regular party "machines."

There have been times when it is to be feared that there has been corruption in Boston's municipal representation, fostered by great corporate interests which had something to get from the city, either in contracts or franchises. There is no doubt that in the expenditure of the public money there has been a great deal of culpable extravagance and unpardonable waste, and that more money has been spent again and again than the result justified. But there has never been any plundering of the city treasury; and the municipal history of Boston has not been disgraced yet by such robberies as were familiar to New York under the government of Tweed. Of late, after a period of steady decline in character and efficiency, the tendency despite many fluctuations has seemed to be upward rather than downward, and in the direction of improvement in the system and methods of administration rather than the reverse. The wise movement which has gained supporters in every American state and city, and which aims to concentrate responsibility and make the city officers more directly answerable to the people, has grown in force, and has found expression in practical amendments to the city charter. But no provision of law, however wise, can of itself secure good government. If the democratic system is to succeed, it must be through the people themselves; and in large cities this success can be secured only by the hardest and most diligent political work on the part of the most intelligent citizens and of those most interested in the welfare of the city. Even then it is certain that under the difficulties of modern conditions we shall fall far short of perfection; but without this effort on the part of all honest citizens, it is sure beyond a peradventure that the course will be downward, until a point is reached that will seriously imperil the welfare of any city.

The problems of governing a great city are many and various. Boston had forty thousand inhabitants when she gave up her town government. She has today within her city limits nearly half a million of people, while in her suburbs, which really form part of the daily life of the municipality, are gathered half a million more. When the town became a city it had a debt of $100,000, and the current expenses for 1822 were $249,000. December 31, 1890 the net city debt was thirty-one millions, the valuation nearly eight hundred millions, and the annual expenditure for the last fiscal year nearly eighteen millions. With the difficulties arising from this growth of population and from the expenditures indicated by these figures, as well as from the influx of a large foreign immigration, Boston has on the whole coped successfully. Her municipal government, as has been said, has been very far from ideally perfect; but on the whole it has been fairly successful, and there seems to be a popular disposition to realize the importance of changes which new conditions necessitate.

In the sixty-eight years which have elapsed since the city charter first went into effect, that part of the history of Boston which is most interesting is not disclosed by a catalogue of her improvements in street paving and drainage, in the introduction of gas, water, horse railroads and electric lighting, nor by the dry annals and ordinances of succeeding city governments. That which is of real value in the events of that period is to be found in the history of the changes which have been wrought in population and in public opinion, and in tracing the development of thought and of hereditary tendencies and their modifications through the introduction of new elements and conditions.

When the town became a city it had a debt of $100,000, and the current expenses for 1822 were $249,000.

There was no part of the United States, during the colonial time, in which there was so little mixture of races as in New England. Dr. Palfrey says, in his History of New England, that for a hundred and fifty years there was practically no admixture of blood with the English stock which first settled the country; and that there was probably no part of the dominion of Great Britain where the English race could be found in greater purity than in the Puritan colonies. New England was settled by a large emigration of Puritan Englishmen. After the first rush had ended, her territory was gradually occupied by the descendants of the early settlers, and by men of the same sort who continued to come from year to year, although in smaller numbers than at first, from the mother-country. Toward the end of the seventeenth century there was a small Huguenot emigration to New England, as to most of the English colonies in America; and of all the many strains of blood in the new world none has proved better than that of these French refugees. They assimilated almost immediately with the English inhabitants, and by their thrift and industry as well as by their strength of character and their ability, held an important place in the community which their descendants have always retained. They were too few, however, in number to have any very marked effect on the population of which they became a part. To New Hampshire there came also a small emigration from the north of Ireland,—men and women of Scotch blood or descended from Cromwell's soldiers, stanch Protestants who had made themselves famous by the great defence of Londonderry, and known in the United States as the Scotch-Irish. Wherever these people went they played an important part, and their names may be found in the history of New Hampshire and of Massachusetts, occupying conspicuous places both in peace and war. But this emigration, like that of the Huguenots, was too small to have any very definite influence upon the general character of the population, and was scarcely perceptible outside of New Hampshire.

To a degree, of course, Boston differed from the rest of New England in the fact that it was a large town given up to trade and commerce, and like all busy seaports had drawn to itself a certain floating population from which were recruited the mobs of the Revolution, who so often troubled the patriot leaders by their unseasonable outbreaks. But here again it may be said, as in the case of the Huguenots and the Scotch-Irish, that this floating population was too small to have any marked influence upon the great body of the population of the town. It was not until Boston had become a city, and had entered upon the third century of its existence, that the great change in its population began. This change has gone on at an accelerated pace to the present day, until now more than half the population is of either foreign birth or parentage. This immigration does not represent the wide variety

It was not until Boston had become a city, and had entered upon the third century of its existence, that the great change in its population began.

so noticeable in the case of New York. There have come to Boston, of course, men of different race stocks. There are Scotch, English, Germans, Scandinavians, Italians, and Portuguese among her foreign-born population, as there would be in almost any large city; but all these elements are numerically small. The great bulk of the immigration which has come to Boston and remained there, has been from Ireland; and it is the Irish who compose the vast mass of those people of foreign birth and parentage who now outnumber the original possessors of the city.

The process of assimilation which has gone on all over the United States, by which men of so many different races have been turned into good American citizens, and by which also an American type has been developed, has of course been at work in

New England and in Boston as well as elsewhere. The people of New England, however, have taken less kindly to the foreign infusion, and assimilated it less readily, than has been the case generally in other parts of the United States. This was due partly to the fact that the New Englanders had lived for so many years with scarcely any foreign admixture, and partly to the deeply imprinted and avowed belief of the early Puritans that they were a chosen people, set apart from the rest of mankind for a particular work in the world.

We are always slow to realize the endurance of defined traditions and habits of thought. Where these traditions and habits come from a people of such marked qualities and rigid beliefs as were possessed by the men who first settled New England, their influence and endurance are even greater than usual. More interesting, however, than pride of race has been the development of the early Puritan qualities of thought under modern conditions. In the earlier chapters of this volume I have pointed out the conflict which all unconsciously the Puritans planted in Boston, when they established a narrow theocracy as the government of a united Church and State, and then placed on one side of it political liberty, and on the other the free school. Yet the very incongruity of this combination typified the Puritan himself.

He was primarily a reformer, a man who thought for himself, and who accepted nothing as necessarily right simply because it was established. He was a man in fact who revolted against the established order of things in the state if it seemed to him wrong, and who refused to think in religion as the Church ordered him to think. Set free from all bonds in a new country, he followed the dictates of that imperious will which is the inseparable companion of the strong characters, by setting up his iron theocracy with one hand, while with the other he followed the opposite impulse of his nature, and struck off the fetters from the human mind. He did not himself see the incongruity of this arrangement; but events soon developed it, and in the inevitable conflict which followed, the theocracy went down.

Nevertheless, although the power of the churches under the law broke down, the clergy continued for another century to exercise an enormous influence both socially and politically. They were the learned class, and they were besides a vigorous body of men. Naturally conservative, they nevertheless, with hardly an exception, espoused the patriot side at the period of the Revolution, because England among her many blunders had given them reason to believe that she contemplated the establishment of Episcopacy in Massachusetts. This was one principal cause of the fact that outside of Boston there were hardly any Tories. The other colonies, with the exception of Virginia, were divided, as is the case in all civil wars; but in those of New England all men practically were on the side of revolution, and this may be largely attributed to the influence of the clergy. After the adoption of the constitution, the ministers of New England went back to their normal position of conservatism and the support of energetic government. Almost to a man they were in favour of the constitution, and stanch Federalists. It was owing in large measure to their teachings that the people of Massachusetts regarded the mild

The Puritan was primarily a reformer, a man who thought for himself, and who accepted nothing as necessarily right simply because it was established.

Jefferson as little better than an American Robespierre, and clung so tenaciously to Federalism long after the rest of the country had abandoned it. But even then the end was at hand. The intellectual movement which began at the close of the eighteenth century could neither be stopped nor excluded, and there was a general revolt against the influence and the doctrines of the churches founded by Winthrop and his followers.

The Puritans belonged to that class of Englishmen who began by reasoning themselves first out of the Roman Catholic Church, and next out of the Church of England. At the end of the seventeenth century their effort to repress dissent in Massachusetts by law, which they carried as far as the imposition of the death penalty, broke down completely. Then came a period of quiet; and then at the end of the next century the second movement set in, and a large portion of the descendants of the Puritans reasoned themselves away from their own doctrines. In Connecticut the division led to a political revolution. In Massachusetts the churches lost the taxes imposed for their benefit by the state, and separated into the Unitarian and Trinitarian Congregationalists. The new movement found its headquarters in Boston, and its most brilliant representative in William Ellery Channing. The old faith held out better in the country, but in the city fashion declared for the Unitarians, who for many years were the ruling sect in Boston. The movement, of course, did not stop at Unitarianism. It produced not only Channing but Theodore Parker, and gave birth to Transcendentalism and other speculative doctrines in which a period of religious restlessness is sure to be prolific. The outward forms and customs, as is apt to be the case, died harder than the vital principles. Long after the stern faith of the forefathers had drifted far away, the habits of much church-going, of gloomy observance of Sunday, and of keen suspicion of all that was amusing still endured. These in their turn have faded, although the Puritan Sabbath, despite much modification, still holds sway in the United States as in England.

The breaking down of the old ecclesiastical system, however, had many results even more important than those in the field of religion itself. From the beginning there had been great intellectual activity among the people who founded Boston and settled Massachusetts; but this activity for many generations was confined to religion and politics. Outside these two subjects the mental energy of the people was devoted to the hard struggle, first for existence, and then for material prosperity. In both they were abundantly successful. At the time of the Revolution Boston was one of the most thriving towns in all his Majesty's dominions. Then came the siege, with disaster and decline in its train. But the town soon recovered from the check it then received, and after the adoption of the constitution its prosperity advanced again at quickened pace.

The foundation of the wealth of Boston was in commerce; and this which had built it up in colonial days, received an enormous extension during the wars which succeeded the French Revolution, and which gradually drove almost all neutral flags but that of the United States from the seas. The people of New England took speedy advantage of their opportunity, and New England vessels penetrated into every part of the globe and grasped the commerce which their rivals had been compelled to abandon. They very nearly absorbed the carrying trade of the world; and it was owing to their wonderful success and corresponding profits that the trouble began between the United States and England which culminated in the war of 1812. In the first decade of the century a Salem merchant was said to be the largest ship-owner in the world, and he was but a type of a class whose headquarters were at Boston.

Jefferson's and Madison's embargoes, however, followed by the war of 1812, forced Boston investments into another channel, that of manufactures and in enterprise. The war, which in effect was a prohibitory tariff, was followed by tariff laws avowedly for the purpose of protection; and the movement of business toward domestic industry gained rapidly in strength and volume. On the new field thus opened, Boston capital soon reaped even larger rewards than it had ever gained upon the ocean. With the invention of the locomotive the business of Boston took still another turn; and the surplus capital accumulated in commerce and manufactures began to pour into railroads, and at a still later time to go out in large masses for the development of the West in all possible directions. The outcome of this has been an enormous accumulation of capital in Massachusetts; for despite the many losses that were certain to come from so many new undertakings the general result has been one of great profit, and the wealth of the modern city and of the State has thus been raised to a point exceeding that of all but one or two of the States of the Union. This accumulation of capital and growth of wealth which began at the opening of the present century, coupled with the decline of the old religious severity, gave scope also for intellectual development in fields hitherto untried. To one class this great business prosperity brought leisure, and to another it promised rewards for success in other directions than trade, politics, or religion. In the early days

With the disappearance of the notion that learning was the special attribute of the clergy, the literary talents of the people took on a broad expansion.

the clergy had been the one educated class, and it was for their especial benefit that Harvard College had been founded. Now the professions of law and medicine rose into prominence, and offered careers and prizes which had been before unknown.

Literature from the beginning had a firm foothold in New England, and in the eighteenth century was far more considerable and important than in the other colonies. It was during this period that the literary genius of Massachusetts produced Jonathan Edwards's remarkable essay on "The Freedom of the Will," Franklin's "Poor Richard," and the rhymes of "Mother Goose," usually attributed to Thomas Fleet of Boston. These were works which differed widely in character and importance, but they all had the quality which gives a place in the literature of the world. The mass of Puritan literature however was extensive rather than important, and was confined almost exclusively to local history and religious tracts. In the nineteenth century all this changed. With the widening in the number of pursuits, and with the disappearance of the notion that learning was the special attribute of the clergy, the literary talents of the people took on a broad expansion. To the first half of the nineteenth century belong in the field of history Bancroft, Prescott, Motley, and a little later Parkman; then there were besides Hawthorne, Longfellow, Whittier, Holmes, Emerson, and Lowell. This group of men, whose writings now form a part of the great literature of the English-speaking people, gathered naturally in Boston and gave it its literary reputation, bringing at the same time in their train many less distinguished writers, who have contributed to spread New England thought throughout the continent.

The purely intellectual development in literature and the learned professions, when freed from the trammels of the earlier civilization, went forward much more rapidly than that which was more affected by the customs and habits of daily life. Amusements were of slow growth in Puritan soil. The theatre, despite Governor Hancock, came in, as has been said, at the close of the eighteenth century, but it was not till fifty years later that it became thoroughly established; and since then, curiously enough, Boston has been reputed to have in proportion to its size the largest population of theatre-goers in the United States. Art was of slower growth, although the prejudice against it was less strong than against the theatre. Copley and Stuart were great names of the earlier days, and since their time artists have slowly increased in number; but it has not been until the last twenty years that a Museum of Art could be established and find strength to thrive in Boston. Music was another of the arts held in little favour by the Puritans, who never seem to have carried it much beyond that stage of devotional harmony represented by "leaders" and "lining." With the present century, however, the love of music and the interest in it have had a great and rapid

development in Boston, and today it is second only to New York
in this field, while the contribution of Massachusetts to the
musicians of reputation in the country has been larger than that
of any other state.

In this way, in law and in medicine, in literature and in art, as
well as in other directions, there was a quick expansion when the
freedom which came in the early years of the nineteenth century
gave at last ample scope for the mental energy and versatility of
the New England people. In these respects, however, the change
sprang merely from the liberation of thought effected by the
decline of the religious system of the Puritans. The actual conflict
between the contending principles which they planted is best
seen, and can be fully realized, only in the great field of public
questions, upon which the history of both State and Nation has
turned during the present century.

The defect of the Puritan,—and he stamped deep upon his
State, his church, and his descendants all his qualities good and
bad,—the defect of the Puritan is obvious enough to any one.
He had an intense faith, beside which the beliefs of the present

day look pale and colourless; he was a bold soldier and a sagacious politician; he was as industrious in worldly affairs as he was fervent in spiritual things; and his worldly prosperity rose as high as energy and thrift could build it. His standard of morals was lofty, his view of life and its responsibilities was serious. Where he failed was in that tolerance and breadth of mind which are more common in modern days than they were in his. He saw clearly and plainly but he saw narrowly; he was rigid, harsh, and often relentless and unforgiving. The lighter side of life, which breeds liberality of opinion more quickly than anything else, was an abomination to the Puritans of the days of Laud and Cromwell. The existence which they led may have been satisfactory to their spiritual wants, but in every other way it was grim and narrow to the last degree. As years went by and the descendants of the original Puritans grew more liberal, their manners softened; and as has been already pointed out, the fine arts and the pleasures of life came in. The leading qualities of the Puritan character and belief, which they had impressed upon State and Church and society alike, were thus softened and modified; but they still cropped out with unvarying regularity whenever occasion served. If we study the phases of public opinion in Boston during some of her seventy years of city government, we shall find, if we look rightly, the reforming spirit of the Puritan always ready to revolt against established things if they seemed unrighteous, and side by side with it the intolerant narrowness of the early theocracy and its followers.

After the Federalists disappeared, the political party which was dominant in Massachusetts and in Boston, and which furnished mayors and aldermen to the city, was the Whig party, eminently conservative and respectable, interested in tariffs and internal improvements and averse to all forms of agitation. Yet it was during that very quiet and highly respectable time that the Antislavery movement began. There in Boston could be seen, as any one might have predicted who knew the history of the people, the two Puritan principles again in active conflict. It was to Boston that Garrison came a poor, unaided young man, to begin his warfare against slavery. It was in the streets of Boston that he was assailed by a mob, which contemporary authority tells us was made up of persons of property and standing; and it is also in a Boston street that his statue stands today to bear witness to his deeds. It was there a few years later that Phillips made his great speech on the Lovejoy murder; and then, so far as was possible, was ostracized in consequence of it and of his further support of Abolition principles, from the society in which his family had long been honoured.

It may be said, and with a great deal of truth, that however righteous such men as Garrison and Phillips may have been they were fanatics of an extreme type, with whom society could not at the beginning be expected to have sympathy. They were doing their work, and a great work, in arousing the conscience of the country; but they offered no practical solution of the terrible problem of slavery, and their doctrines seemed to threaten the subversion of law and order, and of the union of the States. But if excuses can be found for Boston society in this respect, no such defence can be made for its conduct toward those who were fighting the same battle as Garrison and Phillips within the limits of the Constitution, along well-trodden paths, and by methods which if slower than those of the Abolitionists had the merit of being both lawful and effective. It was at this very period that John Quincy Adams, single-handed and alone, began in behalf of the right of petition the great constitutional battle against slavery, which culminated thirty years later in the election of Lincoln, the Civil War, and the Emancipation of the slaves, as Adams had foreseen, through the war powers of the Constitution. How was this lawful and constitutional champion of free speech dealt with by the men who felt that they were entitled to lead in Boston by right of intelligence, wealth, and inheritance? For an answer

I quote the words of Mr. Adams's biographer, Mr. John T. Morse, who states the case most admirably:—

> At home Mr. Adams had not the countenance of that class in society to which he naturally belonged. A second time he found the chief part of the gentlemen of Boston and its vicinity,—the leading lawyers, the rich merchants, the successful manufacturers,—not only opposed to him, but entertaining towards him sentiments of personal dislike and even vindictiveness. This stratum of the community having a natural distaste for disquieting agitation, and influenced by class feeling,—the gentlemen of the North sympathizing with the aristocracy of the South,—could not make common cause with the Antislavery people. Fortunately, however, Mr. Adams was returned by a country district where the old Puritan instincts were still strong. The intelligence and free spirit of New England were at his back, and were fairly represented by him; in spite of high-bred disfavor they carried him gallantly through the long struggle. The people of the Plymouth district sent him back to the House every two years from the time of his first election to the day of his death,

and the disgust of the gentlemen of Boston was after all of trifling consequence to him, and of no serious influence upon the course of history. The old New England instinct was in him as it was in the mass of the people; that instinct made him the real exponent of New England thought, belief, and feeling, and that same instinct made the great body of voters stand by him with unswerving constancy. When his fellow representatives almost to a man deserted him, he was sustained by many a token of sympathy and admiration coming from among the people at large. Time and the history of the United States have been his potent vindicators. The conservative, conscienceless respectability of wealth was, as is usually the case with it in the annals of the Anglo-Saxon race, quite in the wrong, and predestined to well-merited defeat. It adds to the honor due to Mr. Adams that his sense of right was true enough, and that his vision was clear enough to lead him out of that strong thraldom which class feelings, traditions, and comradeship are wont to exercise.

Much the same fate was meted out to those who trod in Mr. Adams's footsteps. His own son, Charles Francis Adams, and

Sumner, Palfrey, and all the other early Free Soilers fared little better than the Abolitionists at the hands of Boston society. When Richard H. Dana defended the fugitive slaves with a noble disregard of personal consequences, and rendered with no little personal peril a service to humanity which has given his name an honoured place in our history, he was frowned on and rebuked by that portion of the community in which he had been born and brought up, and which esteemed itself the best. These same people in large part went, as was quite natural, with Daniel Webster. When the great statesman on March 7 "made the great refusal," some of his followers in Boston broke away; but the majority remained unmoved. Even in 1860 the society of Boston which had wealth, education, and lineage lagged for the most part far behind the rest of New England, just as they did in the days preceding the Revolution. Despite all that had happened they were still averse to agitation, and still hostile to the Antislavery movement. They satisfied their political consciences by voting for Bell and Everett,— the most meaningless of tickets, supported by the remnant of the Whigs, and with no practical value except respectability. But while they hesitated, the body of the people in Boston and elsewhere had been roused against the wrong of human slavery, as they had been roused against other wrongs of old time. The sight of Sims and Burns forced back into slavery through the streets of Boston awakened a fierce spirit of resistance among the New England people which the majority of respectable society in Boston failed to understand, and with which it was unable to cope.

Thus the Antislavery struggle went on its way in the city as the earlier struggle to suppress the Quakers had gone on in the town. When the war came, the old Puritan spirit rose high and strong and the people of Boston and Massachusetts gave their blood and treasure without stint in defence of the Union. Then the principle which was right triumphed, the war was fought to a victorious end, slavery perished, and the Union was saved. Early in these eventful years, and after a brief season of silence and meditation, respectable Boston came to the conclusion that it had never stoned the prophets, and in reality had been always against slavery, which now had joined itself with disunion. Once convinced of these facts they quietly joined the majority party, and proceeded for the most part to bear their share in saving the country.

We see the old Puritan spirit of repression cropping out among a very different class of people in the sacking and burning of the Ursuline Convent at Charlestown, in the days when Roman Catholicism was still new in Boston, and when a nunnery filled the minds of the Boston teamsters with horror and alarm. We see another expression of it in a wholly different way, and from an entirely different point of view, in the prosecution of Abner Kneeland for blasphemy, because he published a free-thinking paper called the "Investigator," having reasoned himself in Puritan fashion from one church into another more liberal, until at last he reasoned himself out of any church at all.

Incidents like these, now well-nigh forgotten, although not more than half a century old, show the endurance of the early traits, and also their modification and change with the advance of years and the experience of defeat.

As I have already said, the great defect of the early Puritans was their bitter intolerance of differences of opinion. They were no worse in this respect than most of the people of that time. They were probably indeed somewhat better; for they had other and ameliorating sides. But harsh narrowness was conspicuous in their characters; and if a man differed from them on a religious point, which was then the subject that alone absorbed their thoughts, they beat and imprisoned him, and in some cases hanged him, until finally that particular form of intolerance and repression utterly broke down. It appears and reappears again and again, sometimes on great matters, sometimes on small; milder too at each coming, but always with the familiar features. It was the repressive spirit of the early Puritans which visited condign political and social punishment upon John Quincy Adams, because in 1808 he dared to differ from the all-powerful Federalists of Boston. History has vindicated his position; but it matters not whether he was right or wrong. The ruling class in Boston treated him for a difference of opinion on a public question, and for his attitude toward a certain public man, as he would have deserved to have been treated if he had committed some dishonourable or criminal act. This was an almost purely personal matter; but it was the same spirit which urged the mob against Garrison, and which drove Phillips and Sumner, Palfrey, Dana, and others, for the time being, out of that portion of the population which was pleased to call itself society.

Closely joined with the defect was a foible. The defect was intolerance; the foible was respectability. All readers of novels will remember the character of Mrs. Catherick in the "Woman in White," the one ambition of whose disreputable life, turned on the surface to better things, was to secure a recognition of her hard-earned respectability by having the clergyman bow to her as she sat at her window. Wilkie Collins, when he drew this character, displayed in evil and repulsive form the foible for respectability and for conformity to certain standards so deeply rooted among the English-speaking people everywhere. The picture was grossly exaggerated, but nowhere else could he have found that curious mania which Carlyle held up to the jeers of the world as "Gigmanity." It is a laudable thing to be respectable; and the love of respectability is an altogether innocent and commendable passion. It is a very weak thing, on the other hand, to sacrifice one's opinions because persons who set themselves up as respectable do not think these opinions consonant with what they choose to call respectability.

The foibles of the Puritan like his defects, however, have so faded and weakened in the present day that they are hardly visible. Yet his intolerance is an instinct which has never died, and is a curious example of the enormous strength of heredity, especially in a vigorous race. It is very feeble now, and is rather ludicrous than otherwise; but it is still there. It was an extremely real and dangerous thing in earlier times, when it meant something. At the present day it is no longer dangerous; and when it ceased to be formidable, it lost its only claim to consideration. The mastodon would have been an extremely terrible animal to meet; but we can afford to regard its bones with curiosity, and to look upon its footprints in the limestone with a smile.

Such in one direction has been the fate of that stern spirit which placed Cromwell on the throne of England and founded the Puritan commonwealths in America. We can pardon in a man of Cromwell's day an intolerance which was characteristic of the times, and which he was ever ready to back up with the sword; but when it shows itself in its modern form, there is nothing in it to be admired. It is an heir-loom which might better be consigned to the dust-heap. It is fast finding its way there; yet it still lives on,—an interesting feature in the society of the great city which has arisen where the Puritan town once stood. It has fallen far, and is now nothing more than a little mild parochialism. The foible for respectability and the intolerance of differences of opinion

Woe to the daring inhabitant of that parish who ventures to differ from the authorities. He shall not sit in the vestry, nor shall he ever become a beadle.

have come down to a feeling of distrust and an attitude of coldness toward all those who do not agree with the controlling view of the moment in the parish. Even yet we have not grown up so far as to be rid of our awe of the beadle and the vestryman. There are many who cannot yet look far enough into the world beyond to see that our beadle and his vestrymen are really not very important outside the parish bounds. Woe, however, to the daring inhabitant of that parish who ventures to differ from the authorities. He shall not sit in the vestry, nor shall he ever become a beadle.

The sense of the debt due from each man to the commonwealth still holds sway.

Yet after all, the foible and the defect which the Puritans bequeathed to their descendants have been sinking and fading more and more with each succeeding year; and have been replaced by a wider toleration and a more generous treatment of other men, for the love of freedom and hatred of wrong ingrained in the Puritan are always sure to gain the mastery in the end. At the same time the other qualities which made the Puritan great and powerful among men in his day and generation, have as yet neither faded nor weakened. They have been the secret of the success which Boston has gained, and of the services which her people have been able to render to their State and to the Union. The virtues of the Puritan, like his defects, have changed as everything must change. They have progressed because everything has progressed; but they have not died out, as those persons who hold to the good-old-times view of life would have us believe. The love of country and of race is still powerful. The public spirit which was born of membership in a State where religion was the test of citizenship, is still vigorous. The sense of the debt due from each man to the commonwealth still holds sway.

We can see this sense of responsibility in the matter of public benefactions. The Puritan was not naturally an open-handed man with money, for he earned it with difficulty and knew its value; but yet he never failed to do his duty to the public in this respect. Compared with the wealth of modern times, the gifts of John Harvard and the gift of the Bay Colony to the college at Cambridge were the most munificent ever consecrated in this country to the cause of education. No finer monument was ever reared than the noble university which has grown from these early gifts, made by men clinging to the edge of the wilderness two hundred and fifty years ago. It stands there a perpetual and living record of the Puritan belief in education, and of that public spirit which is not only generous but wise. The city of Boston has never faltered in the path that John Harvard marked out and the great college today is the best proof that the Puritan virtues have lived on in their descendants, and that the higher education as well as the public school have been as dear to the sons as they were to the fathers. It is this same public spirit which has filled Boston with noble charities, with hospitals and libraries, and with every kind of institution for the benefit of those to whom fortune has not been as kind as to her favoured few. It was the independent spirit of the Puritans, who refused submission in matters of conscience to the Church, either of Rome or England, which placed Boston and Massachusetts first among the communities of the colonies that raised the standard of revolution against England; and again, first of the communities of the United States which set their faces against the extension, and then against the existence, of slavery. It was the Puritan love of learning which for generations has made a college training the ambition of every thoughtful boy in New England, and which has caused many families to pinch and save, as did the Scotch peasants, so that the eldest born might go to the University. The energy and fearless spirit of the Puritans which brought them to the shores of the new world at the beginning of the seventeenth century, in later times have sent them out in swarms from the parent hive to settle in new States, and have carried Boston capital into the lands of the West, to be returned to the farsighted enterprise of its possessors a thousand fold.

That the picture is all rose-coloured, no sensible man would pretend. That Boston, like other cities, has her dangers to be confronted and her difficulties to be overcome, every one knows; but on the whole she has been true to her traditions. There have been ups and downs; but she has never wholly lost sight of her responsibilities, for the great body of her people has always been sound at heart. Her society has never yet been dominated by mere wealth, although the fortunes of the present day are so great that they are threatening to bring this result, as they have done in other cities. The great struggle for the preservation of the Union showed that the fighting spirit of the Puritans lived on in their children, and that their patriotism and devotion to a great cause were as pure and strong as they had ever been, and as capable of heroism and sacrifice. What the future may bring no man can tell. Great and difficult problems confront this generation and the next; and Boston has her share in them, and in the fate of the mighty empire of which she is a part. The path is beset with difficulties and dangers; but if the city founded by the Puritans is only true to her traditions, she may face what is yet to be with confidence, and have faith that she can overcome the perils of the future as she has prevailed over those of the past.

Picture Credits

Our thanks to the following for permission to reprint images from their collections. The images appear at the beginning of each chapter and have been reproduced in a duotone process.

Chapters 1 and 8 (pages viii and 118): Picture Collection, The Branch Libraries, The New York Public Library, Astor, Lenox and Tilden Foundations.

Chapters 2, 6, 7, 10 and 11 (pages 20, 80, 100, 174 and 204): Courtesy of the Boston Public Library, Print Department.

Chapter 3 (page 36): I. N. Phelps Stokes Collection, Miriam and Ira D. Wallach Division of Art, Prints and Photographs, The New York Public Library, Astor, Lenox and Tilden Foundations.

Chapters 4 and 9 (pages 50 and 142): Boston Athenaeum.

Chapter 5 (page 66) and the cover: Courtesy of the Library of Congress. The image on the cover is taken from a mid-nineteenth century engraving titled "View from steeple of Arlington-Street Church."

Acknowledgments

Many Bostonians and near-Bostonians are to thank, starting with Mandy Young and Rosanne Saleh, our own good pilgrims.

We knocked on numerous doors in our search for old drawings and engravings. Aaron Schmidt and Eric Frazier of the Boston Public Library, Stephan Saks of the New York Public Library, and Patricia Boulos and Catharina Slautterback of the Boston Athenaeum went out of their way to help us mine their archives.

Even where we didn't find a picture, we found helpful and gracious staff members—Sally Hinkle at the Society for the Preservation of New England Antiquities, Debby Curry at the Old North Church, Nancy Richard and Sylvia Weedman at the Bostonian Society, Terri Tremblay at the American Antiquarian Society, Kimberly Nusco at the Massachusetts Historical Society and Leslie Wilson at the Concord Free Public Library.

Others in this *Boston* circle to whom we owe our thanks: Luise Erdmann, Alex Farquharson and Stewart Young.

Special thanks to Paul C. Cabot III for checking us on his family's genealogy. We're so glad that his ancestors decided to make Boston their hub.

Uncommon Books for Serious Readers

Feeding the Mind
by Lewis Carroll

A Fortnight in the Wilderness
by Alexis de Tocqueville

Painting as a Pastime
by Winston S. Churchill

Rare Words
and ways to master
their meanings
by Jan Leighton
and Hallie Leighton

Samuel Johnson's Dictionary
Selections from the 1755 work
that defined the English language
Edited by Jack Lynch

Samuel Johnson's Insults
Edited by Jack Lynch

The Silverado Squatters
Six selected chapters
by Robert Louis Stevenson

**Sir Winston Churchill's Life
Through His Paintings**
by David Coombs
with Minnie Churchill
Foreword by Mary Soames

Words That Make a Difference
and how to use them
in a masterly way
by Robert Greenman

Levenger Press is the publishing arm of

LEVENGER®
TOOLS FOR SERIOUS READERS

www.Levenger.com   800-544-0880

LEVENGER STORES
Boston   Chicago   Delray Beach

The TOWN of
BOSTON
IN
New England
by
Capt John Bonner
1722

West Hill

Roxbury Flatts

Fox Hill

Garden

Beacon Hill

Powder House
Watch House

COMMON

School

Marsh

Pond

From Town H.
One Mile

Orange Str

Rainford

Goals Garden

Pond Str

Orange Str

Fortification

Hills Wharfe

Scale of ¼ a Mile.

Wind Mill Point

BOSTON: N.E
Planted An. Dom. 1630

A. The Old Church	1690
B. Old North	1650
C. Old South	1660
D. Annabaptist	1680
E. Chh of England	1688
F. Brattle St Church	1699
G. Quakers	1710
H. New North	1714
I. New South	1716
K. French	1716
L. New N.º Brick	1721

EXPLANATION.
a. Town House.
b. Governours House.
c. South Gramar School.
d. North Gramar School.
e. Writing School.
f. Writing School.
g. Alms House.
h. Bridewell.
Streets 42 Lanes 36 Alleys 22
Houses near 3000.
1000 Brick rest Timber.
Near 12000 People.

Great Fires.	Gen.ll Small Pox.
First....1653	First....1640
Second....1676	Second....1660
Third....1679	Third....1677/78
Fourth....1683	Fourth....1689/90
Fifth....1690	Fifth....1702
Sixth....1691	Sixth....1721
Seventh....1702	
Eigth....1711	